W9-DFC-639

the Breath and Spirit of God

BY THIERRY MAERTENS, O.S.B.

Translated by Robert J. Olsen
and Albert J. LaMothe, Jr.

FIDES PUBLISHERS, INC. • NOTRE DAME, IND.

In the same series:

THE BREATH AND SPIRIT OF GOD
FEAST IN HONOR OF YAHWEH
MARY, DAUGHTER OF SION
I AM THE WAY
A KING GAVE A MARRIAGE FEAST

Nihil Obstat:
Louis J. Putz, C.S.C.
University of Notre Dame

Imprimatur:
Leo A. Pursley, D.D.
Bishop of Fort Wayne-South Bend

Originally published by Desclée De Brouwer in Belgium, 1959,
under the title, Le souffle et l'Esprit de Dieu.
Library of Congress Catalog Card Number: 64-23515

Contents

Introduction

Whenever we recite the Creed, we say: "I believe in Jesus Christ, the only Son of God, conceived by the Holy Spirit, born of the Virgin Mary. . . . I believe in the Holy Spirit, who spoke by the prophets." Every time that a bishop confirms a Christian, he appeals to the Holy Spirit: "Spiritus Sanctus superveniat in vos."

What is this Spirit of God mentioned in the Christian profession of faith and conferred by the bishop? We shall try to find the answer by listening to the Spirit's own teaching about Himself, for indeed it is the very Spirit of God who will speak to us in the pages of Holy Scripture:

> For not by will of man was prophecy brought at any time; but holy men of God spoke as they were moved by the Holy Spirit (2 Pet. 1:21).[1]

The Spirit, however, will not be clearly apparent to us as a divine person at the start. The Holy Spirit will first

[1] Cf. 2 Kings 23:2; 2 Esd. 9:30; Acts 28:25; 2 Tim. 3:16.

draw our attention to the natural phenomena which initially reveal the activity of His power in the world. And then He will be revealed in the action which He exercises in the lives of men, whom He inspires and whose whole efficacy is derived from Him. Finally, His divine personality will be revealed by Jesus, and by the new activity which He undertakes within the Church after Pentecost.

We shall see the words "ruah" and "pneuma," meaning "spirit," in Hebrew and Greek respectively, as they continually acquire a more exact and stronger significance. These words appear very often in the Bible. As we come upon texts that mention them, we shall first discover the fundamental laws of the Spirit's action upon the world, and then upon the community that God is seeking to guide unto Himself. We shall note the astonishing consistency of God's action from the earliest period in the history of Israel down through the centuries to the Church of today. And when we have completed our study, we shall have a better understanding of that activity which the Spirit of God is still seeking to exercise upon ourselves and upon the Church.

The history of the Spirit of God and of His revelation in Holy Scripture unfolds in three stages. They can be described under three aspects. The Bible first tells of the breath of God acting upon natural elements and phenomena, and then of the Spirit of God influencing certain men and chosen individuals. Finally, the Holy Spirit Himself is at work in Christ and the Church.

Chapter One

THE BREATH OF GOD

In the first pages of the Bible, the word "ruah," spirit, which later designates the Spirit of God, the third person of the divine family, primarily has the meaning of "breath," in the sense of air in motion, as for instance the breath exhaled or inhaled through the nostrils, or the wind that blows over the surface of the earth.[1]

The corresponding verb "ruh" designates the inhaling of air or breathing deeply of some fragrance. The word "reah," closely related to "ruah," means fragrance, odor.

These related connotations, which may seem unimportant, are however very suggestive. Paul, faithful to his Jewish upbringing, readily associated odor, fragrance and Spirit in referring to the Spirit's ministry (2 Cor. 2:14; 3:18).

Moreover, the *sacrament* of the Spirit of holiness and consecration in the days of the ancient priesthood was already a sweet fragrance, an incense, "compounded by

1 The corresponding root "ruh" is common to a large number of Semitic languages.

the work of the perfumer" (Ex. 30:34-38). And even now it is a holy fragrance which is the sign of the Spirit's coming, the fragrance or holy chrism of Baptism and Confirmation, a fragrance which also accompanies the blessing of sacred vessels and even, in certain Eastern Churches, a newly married couple.

The word "ruah," itself, in the first texts of the Bible, designates both "the breath of the nostrils" and "the wind." It means the breath within man and the breath of air that animates nature. We must not forget these two original meanings, for they will often be used in conjunction. They must be kept clearly in mind even when God will have given "ruah" a much deeper significance.

A

the "Breath" of the Wind

1. THE WIND AND NATURE

The word "ruah," especially as we find it in the oldest texts, most often designates the wind, a breath of air. It is in this sense that the author of Genesis 3:8, a text commonly attributed to the Yahweh tradition, shows us God walking in the garden of paradise in "the afternoon air."

All those engaged in the cultivation of land, especially in the oriental countries, are concerned about the winds. It is in fact the wind that conditions the whole existence of the peasant or the nomadic shepherd. It is the wind of the west which brings rain and wealth to a country without water (3 Kings 18:44-45; cf. Luke 12:54). It is the raging wind of a storm that sweeps up and scatters afar the good earth of the fields, burning the crops or devastating everything before it.[2] It is the wind that gathers or disperses the clouds. Accordingly, in the time of Elias, during the reign of the faithless King Achab, God put an end to the great drought in response to the prophet's prayer:

> And while he turned himself this way and that way, behold, the heavens grew dark, with clouds, and wind, and there fell a great rain (3 Kings 18:45).[3]

In the time of Eliseus, however, God ended the drought, although there was no wind at all:

> You shall not see wind, nor rain: and yet this channel shall be filled with waters, and you shall drink, you and your families, and your beasts (4 Kings 3:17).

When the priestly writer, remembering the east wind that blows from the desert,[4] described the primeval chaos, he used the two related ideas of wind and emptiness among the harsh terms of his description:

> And the earth was void and empty, and darkness was upon the face of the deep; and the spirit [i.e. the breath] of God moved over the waters (Gen. 1:2).

This association of wind and desert, although wholly material, must not be forgotten. When the Bible describes

[2] Ex. 10:12-13; Jer. 4:11; 13:24; 18:17; Jon. 4:8; Job 1:19; Is. 28:8; 40:7; Ps. 47:8; Osee 13:15.

[3] We shall have occasion to return to this link between "breath" and "water," cf. p. 48.

[4] Cf. Th. Maertens, *Les Sept Jours,* Editions de l'Abbaye de Saint-André, 1951, pp. 14-25.

the action of the Spirit of God upon the world, we shall often have occasion to note that the wind and the desert serve respectively as the instrument and the setting for this divine activity. For example, when the desert wind divided the waters of the Red Sea, allowing the Hebrews to cross without wetting their feet in a miracle of deliverance, God used the wind as an instrument of His plan of salvation (Ex. 14:21; cf. Gen. 8:1).

Even in the completely spiritual activity of the Holy Spirit, it is still the wind that serves as a term of comparison to help us understand the Spirit's mode of action. We find this, for instance, in Jesus' discussion with Nicodemus regarding the mystery of the new birth:

> The wind blows where it will, and thou hearest its sound but dost not know where it comes from or where it goes. So is everyone who is born of the Spirit (John 3:8).[5]

2. THE MASTER OF THE WIND

Impressed by the power of the capricious wind that brought either wealth or distress, the Semites were often tempted to offer real worship to it. The Chosen People were saved from this pitfall by the covenant concluded with the personal God of Abraham, Isaac, and Jacob. They did not regard the wind as an autonomous divinity, but rather as a force governed and controlled by Yahweh.[6] The winds were considered as so completely be-

[5] Cf. Prov. 2:5. This is the same word which, in the Greek text of St. John, designates both "Wind" and "Spirit."

[6] Gen. 8:1; Ex. 10:13:19; 14:21; Num. 11:31.

longing to God that they were described as "the breath of his own mouth" (Job 15:30).

This recognition of God's control over the winds perhaps accounts for the initial use of the term "Ruah Elohim," "Ruah Yahweh,"[7] the wind of God, the wind of Yahweh which, however, originally designated only the wind, but not the Spirit of God. This expression meant the wind that comes from God, or rather a wind that is particularly violent and truly divine, a wind that is wholly unusual (Osee 13:15 and doubtless Gen. 1:2).

The prophets and psalmists of Israel delighted in saying that God "createth the wind" (Amos 4:13; Nah. 1:3), making use of the winds as His messengers (Ps. 103:3-4), bringing them forth out of His treasures (Ps. 134:7; Jer. 10:13; 51:16), and making a weight for them all (Prov. 16:2; Job 28:25).

The winds were even personified, and were depicted as standing before God, ready to obey His commands (Zach. 6:5). The winds constituted the heavenly court. Ezechiel also mentions the "ruah" surrounding God, but this term had by then already acquired the meaning of "spirit" (Ezech. 1). And in the Apocalypse we read of the "spirits" (Apoc. 4:5).

Accordingly, the winds were quite naturally obedient to the commands of Jesus (Matt. 8:26-27), thus helping us to understand that another "Spirit" would come, also at Jesus' command (John 16:7).

[7] 3 Kings 18:12; 4 Kings 2:16; Is. 40:7; 59:19.

3. THE HERALDS OF GOD'S PURPOSE

These "winds of God" accompany all the interventions of the Lord in the course of history. They are present during the resounding theophanies that mark the historical stages of the people of God.

According to the priestly author, it was the wind that brought the cataclysm of the flood to an end (Gen. 8:1), and divided the waters of the sea for the Hebrews (Ex. 14:21-22). When the people of God had assembled at the foot of Mount Sinai, the wind trumpeted, as though summoning the people to gather there:

> And now the third day was come, and the morning appeared: and behold thunders began to be heard, and lightning to flash, and a very thick cloud to cover the mount, and the noise of the trumpet sounded exceeding loud . . . (Ex. 19:16).

When David sang of his own deliverance at the time of Saul's devious intrigues against him, comparing the interventions of God in his own life to the divine intervention in the Passover, he described God as rushing to his assistance on the wings of the wind:

> He bowed the heavens, and came down: and darkness was under his feet. And he rode upon the cherubims, and flew: and slid upon the wings of the wind. And the overflowings of the sea appeared, and the foundations of the world were laid open at the rebuke of the Lord, at the blast of the spirit of his wrath (2 Kings 22:10-16; cf. Ps. 103:3-4).

In the imagery of the poet, the wind or spirit is breathed forth from the nostrils of Yahweh. In this instance it was the spirit of His wrath, but there are other references also. Apart from the breath of Yahweh's anger, there was the gentle air of His friendship that revealed His presence to the prophet Elias on Horeb, even more surely than to Moses:

> . . . behold the Lord passeth, and a great strong wind before the Lord overthrowing the mountains, and breaking the rocks in pieces: the Lord is not in the wind, and after the wind an earthquake: the Lord is not in the earthquake. And after the earthquake a fire: the Lord is not in the fire, and after the fire a whistling of a gentle air. And when Elias heard it, he covered his face with his mantle. . . . and behold a voice unto him . . . (3 Kings 19:11-13).

Psalm 103 depicts the winds as the servants and heralds of God. It is indeed in this role that they appear in a great many texts of the Bible. God uses the winds to accomplish His works for the sake of the people He has chosen.

It was the "wind of God" that brought about and ended the eighth plague of Egypt (Ex. 10:13-19), the clouds of locusts. It was a wind sent forth by God that divided the Red Sea in two, thus ensuring the passage of the Hebrews (Ex. 15:8-10; cf. Is. 11:15). It was a wind raised by God that brought quails to the starving people (Num. 11:31; cf. Ex. 16:13; Ps. 77:27), and then also manna (Ex. 16:13-16; Ps. 77:24-25):

> And a wind going out from the Lord, taking quails up beyond the sea brought them, and cast them into the camp . . . (Num. 11:31).

The wind was there at the moment of the promulgation of the Law, shaking the mountain and whirling around it, in the midst of thunder and lightning (Ex. 19:16-20).

The wind of God in these texts was no longer merely a physical force controlled by Yahweh, but the very instrument of His supernatural action upon the world. Quite possibly it was through the occurrence of the Exodus that the wind acquired the prerogative of being regarded as one of the best of Yahweh's servants. The portrayal of the wind's inconsistency and vanity, although quite as natural, is not very prevalent in biblical literature (cf. Is. 26:18; 41:29; Mich. 2:11; Job 16:3; Jer. 5:13).

4. THE WIND OF VENGEANCE

When they described new interventions of God in history, the prophets remembered the presence of the wind during the first manifestations of God in the saving of His people.

The wind intervened providentially in the forming of the Chosen People, and again at the time of the covenant of Sinai. The prophets were later to attribute to the wind a divine activity when God sought to avenge the covenant violated by His people, or to lead His unfaithful sons back to the way of righteousness:

> A burning wind is in the ways that are in the desert of the way of the daughter of my people. . . . A full wind from these places shall come to me . . . (Jer. 4:11-13).

> . . . the Lord will bring a burning wind that shall rise from the desert, and it shall dry up his springs, and shall make

> his fountain desolate, and he shall carry off the treasure of every desirable vessel (Osee 13:15).

Jeremias described the action of the wind driving the people into captivity:

> The wind shall feed all thy pastors, and thy lovers shall go into captivity . . . (Jer. 22:22).

The terrible wind of the desert assumed an avenging role, punishing unfaithfulness to the covenant.

In the apocalyptic texts, the wind of God which "scatters the wicked like straw in the air," is the instrument of God's vengeance against all nations:

> Thus saith the Lord: Behold I will raise up as it were a pestilential wind against Babylon and against the inhabitants thereof. . . . And I will send to Babylon fanners, and they shall fan her, and shall destroy her land . . . (Jer. 51:1-2).
>
> When thou shalt cry, let thy companies deliver thee, but the wind shall carry them all off, a breeze shall take them away, but he that putteth his trust in me, shall inherit the land, and shall possess my holy mount. (Is. 57:13).[8]

[8] Cf. also Jer. 13:24; 18:17; 49:36; Job 4:9; 30:22; Ezech. 13:11-13; 17:10; 27:26; Osee 4:19; Ps. 1:4; 17:43; 34:5; 106:25; Is. 4:4; 30:28.

B

the Breath of Respiration

1. THE BREATH OF LIFE

Passages in which "ruah" has the meaning of respiration, as breath which passes through the nostrils, are also numerous, but they generally belong to a period less ancient than the texts on the wind. The two meanings, however, have co-existed from the beginning. They are contained in the etymology of the word, and a few texts clearly establish the antiquity of this second meaning.

The breath that is exhaled and inhaled through the nostrils is indispensable to existence itself. It was by breathing into man's face that God conferred life.[9] And

[9] The term employed in Gen. 2:7 is not "ruah" but "nesamah." The latter term, however, did not endure as did "ruah," and when the subsequent writers refer to the account of Gen. 2, they always use "ruah." The two words appear side by side in Job 32:8; 33:4; 34:14.

when God decided to shorten a man's days in this world, He spoke of withdrawing His "ruah" from him (Gen. 6:3).

Considered as the breath of the nostrils, "ruah" always remained associated with the notion of life. Man's existence was closely connected with the coming-and-going of the vital breath. In the Bible, the word "ruah" even appears with the meaning of "life" itself (Mal. 2:15-16).

Man's life, being essentially precarious, constantly depends on a gift that must be renewed every time that he breathes:

> Put not your trust in princes: in the children of men, in whom there is no salvation. His spirit shall go forth, and he shall return into his earth: in that day all their thoughts shall perish (Ps. 145:2-4; cf. 77:39).

And Job extolled God's power and wisdom, speaking of the Lord:

> In whose hand is the soul of every living thing, and the spirit of all flesh of man (Job 12:10).
>
> It is not in man's power to stop the spirit, neither has he power in the day of death . . . (Eccles. 8:8).
>
> And the dust return into its earth, from whence it was, and the spirit return to God, who gave it (Eccles. 12:7).

The realization of this total dependence of man's breath and spirit in relation to God is noted in a particularly forceful way in Psalm 103:27-30.

> All expect of thee that thou give them food in season. What thou givest to them they shall gather up: when thou openest thy hand, they shall all be filled with good. But if thou turnest away thy face, they shall be troubled: thou

> shalt take away their breath, and they shall fail, and shall return to their dust. Thou shalt send forth thy spirit, and they shall be created: and thou shalt renew the face of the earth (cf. also Is. 62:5).

It is in this sense that Yahweh is the "God of the spirits of all mankind," in the splendid language of the priestly tradition (Num. 16:22; 27:16). Similarly, the breath which has animated man may truly be called the "breath of God," as in most of the passages that we have had occasion to quote.

2. A "DIVINE" REALITY

For most of the biblical writers, respiration seemed to be something divine. Job is deserving of praise for having emphasized its origin:

> As long as breath remains in me, and the spirit of God in my nostrils, My lips shall not speak iniquity . . . (Job 27:3-4).
>
> The spirit of God made me, and the breath of the Almighty gave me life (Job 33:4).
>
> If he return his heart to him, he shall draw his spirit and breath unto himself. All flesh shall perish together, and man shall return into ashes (Job 34:14-15).

It is not surprising that the whole of creation is later attributed to the breath of God (Ps. 103:30), and the world's renewal by its creative action. The new creation, with the resurrection of the People of God following the ordeal of exile, was indeed to be, in its turn, the work of the Spirit of God (Ezech. 37).

3. THE BREATH AND THE SOUL

The breath given by God, which enters and leaves the nostrils, engenders and sustains man's life. It is also an expression of it, for a man's breathing teaches us a great deal about his thoughts and feelings and vigor.

It is sometimes said of a man that he takes a long breath, as if to signify his patience and "long-suffering" endurance. If breathing is slow and exhausted, it is a sign of dejection or fear. The Canaanites, for example, "lost their breath" at the approach of the Hebrews (Jos. 2:11; 5:1). And to describe his wretchedness, Job said that his breath or spirit would be broken (17:1).[10] Ardor in battle connotes rapid and short breathing. A great joy revives and rouses the spirit (Gen. 45:27).

The blast of the tyrant was like the whirlwind (Is. 25:4). On the other hand, when anger abated, the "spirit was appeased" (Jdg. 8:3).

The Bible also tells us that the Queen of Sheba lost her breath, having "no longer any spirit in her," when she gazed upon Solomon's splendor (3 Kings 10:5).

In Jewish anthropology the breath of respiration consequently appears as revealing the thoughts and feelings of the soul. The soul was judged by it. And so it became customary to seek out the moral aspect of man's spirit and its relation to the very roots of the soul.

[10] The same expression occurs in Is. 54:6; Ps. 141:4; 142:4; Prov. 15:13.

4. THE "BREATH" AND THE FLESH

We have noted how the wind and the breath of respiration appeared to the Hebrews as realities that were in some sense divine. We must lay stress on this.

For the Hebrews, the wind was a power dependent on the world above. If, perchance, it irrupted in the world here below, it was often merely destructive, although freely creating thereafter:

> The grass is withered, and the flower is fallen: because the spirit of the Lord hath blown upon it (Is. 40:7).

This is also true, even more emphatically, of the breath of respiration, the breath of the nostrils. The latter, according to Father Guillet, is truly "a force too frankly divine to be anything but a borrowed gift, a passing guest in man."[11] The Bible readily contrasts the flesh of which man is made with the spirit that gives him life. The writers of the sapiential books all laid great stress on this.

At death, a man "goes to his lasting home . . ."

> And the dust return into its earth, from whence it was, and the spirit return to God, who gave it (Eccles. 12:7).

Man thus seems to be the precarious composite of two elements, one of which comes from above and the other from below. And Paul's noted contrasting of the "flesh and the spirit" was already deep-rooted in ancient Jewish anthropology (cf. Is. 31:3).

[11] Guillet, *Themes of the Bible,* Notre Dame, Fides, 1960, pp. 243-244.

We see, therefore, that both wind and breath, although wholly material elements, were considered almost from the first as the envoys and heralds of a supernatural world.

It was quite easy to pass, without being aware of it, from wind and breath to the spirit of God, which gradually became evident as the agent of divine activity and the source of inspiration for the prophets. Finally, it was perceived as the Holy Spirit Himself.

Conclusion

In the first stage of revelation concerning the Spirit of God we followed the evolving meaning of the word "ruah" in two different respects. Whether as the wind or as respiration, breath comes from God. It was Yahweh who sent the wind to govern the world and save His people. It was the same Yahweh who sent His other breath to give man life. The breath or spirit of God thus intervenes at the same time both interiorly and exteriorly. This became a constant rule in the action of the spirit of God and of the Holy Spirit.

The breath of God, in these two aspects, was therefore already highly spiritualized. It was the messenger of a supra-material and supernatural world. It was not subject to the laws of this present world. The wind often made those same laws quake, and the breath of life was precariously unstable in human flesh.

Nevertheless, the breath of God is the breath of life, animating the human body and giving water to make the earth fertile. From the very beginning of the semantic evolution of the word "ruah," the association between breath and life was so pronounced that it was to continue so to the highest point of that development: the Holy Spirit of the living God.

But while it gives life, the wind also brings the vengeance of God. It is the instrument of His wrath, and therefore is characteristic of the days of vengeance, and more especially the "last days," as we shall soon see. The same may be said of the breath of respiration. A great deal of "breath" would be needed to accomplish one or another phase of God's plan. The breath of respiration would be particularly necessary in those times when God would finally achieve His purpose in its fullness. At the start, as we see, "ruah" possessed eschatalogical implications that only needed to find expression. And this is what happened in the stage of the "spirit of God."

In conclusion, let us note the moral aspect common to the two breaths of God. Respiration reveals the soul's thoughts and feelings, but it is the wind which brings the Law to the people. Respiration unveils the wickedness of the soul, and it is the wind that punishes.

Its divine origin and its belonging to the mysterious super-terrestrial world, its connection with life, eschatology, and morality, are all essential characteristics of the *ruah* of God. These are the aspects that will guide us in our further study.

the Breath and Spirit of God

Chapter Two

THE SPIRIT OF GOD

Heretofore the breath of God has been described primarily in terms of the wind and the breath of life. But the word "ruah" now becomes gradually spiritualized and acquires a less material meaning. Instead of signifying respiration alone, it becomes the equivalent of spirit, soul, mind, heart.[1]

This word "spirit" will designate, not merely the "winds," but "angels" also, who replace the winds in doing the tasks that God entrusts to them. They are the mysterious spiritual creatures who form the court of the Lord, and whom He uses as "messengers" and servants whenever He wishes to act upon earth.[2]

1 See in Genesis 26:35: "Judith, daughter of Beeri . . . and Basemath, daughter of Elon . . . were a *source of bitterness for* Isaac and Rebecca." (Trans. note: The Confraternity English version here lacks the word "soul" required by the context; the French reads: "bitterness of soul.") Gen. 41:8; Ex. 35:21; 3 Kings 21:5; Job 6:4; Ps. 31:2; 33:19; 142:4.

2 3 Kings 22:19-23; cf. 1 Kings 16:14; 18:10; 19:9; Judges 9:23. The evil spirits themselves appear as servants of God. It is difficult to see to what extent the *evil spirit* is personalized in the text of 1 Kings 16:14 fol., or whether it is just a case, as in Judges 9:23, of a wicked disposition of spirit (Num. 5:14, 30; 4 Kings 19:7; Is. 19:14; 29:10, see Jerusalem Bible, *Les livres de Samuel,* p. 80).

The story of the possession of Saul by an "evil spirit of Yahweh" recalls the cases of possession related in the Gospels.

"Ruah" will finally designate the spirit of God in particular, who dwells in the hearts of men led and inspired by God in special ways, and of whom He makes His prophets.

We must not, however, forget all that we have learned thus far. The spirit acting in the prophets appears at first to be, in some sense, a modification of their own respiration and vital breath. The spirit sometimes also acts like the wind, carrying them along unresistingly. This prophetic spirit, as a source and principle of new life, becomes only gradually apparent. But the later prophets proclaim that "in the last days" it will renew all the races of mankind and the face of the whole world.

A

the Spirit, the Breath of the Prophets

1. THE SUPERNATURAL BREATH

The phenomenon of inspired men of God drew the attention of the biblical authors to particular manifestations of the breath, and later of the spirit, of God.

In especially difficult circumstances, certain heroes displayed a courage that seemed far beyond their own ordinary capacities. A divine breath, the breath of Yahweh Himself, inspired and sustained them, and it gradually became evident that the source was the very spirit of God (see 1 Kings 11:6). It seemed, in fact, that Yahweh had transmitted His own breath to them, for they accomplished such great things that merely human respiration could never keep pace.

It was this "breath of Yahweh" that ensured victory to Gideon (Jdg. 6:34), Jephte (11:29) and Othoniel (3:10). It was this same breath of Yahweh that enabled Samson to defeat the lion in single combat (14:6; 15:14).

Along with military heroes, certain persons in ecstasy, whose excitation was manifested precisely by jerky breathing, seemed possessed by a spirit that was not their own. The Bible tells us that they were under the spell of Yahweh's breath, as when Saul (1 Kings 10:6) and David (19:23) were "possessed" in moments of sudden exaltation, followed by complete and prolonged exhaustion (19:24).

The prophetic spirit appears in the biblical Books of Kings as something essentially contagious, but also as something still more closely resembling the exaltation of pagan prophets (3 Kings 22:10-12, cf. 3 Kings 18, in which the two kinds of prophesying are contrasted). 3 Kings 19:11-13 (Elias' vision on Mount Horeb) is certainly indicative of the transition from one kind of prophesying to another.

In this group of texts a new meaning of the "breath of Yahweh" becomes apparent. Much more distinctly than in the past, it connoted a superhuman power enabling men to perform deeds that surpassed the normal powers of mankind.

The earlier writers depict this power as descending upon inspired men or heroes to make "spiritual men" of them (Osee 9:7), but they do not yet fully realize that it was capable of transforming man interiorly, in a permanent way, conferring a wholly new personality upon him.

Nevertheless, the passage in the Book of Samuel (1 Kings) in which the prophet announces the sudden descent of Yahweh's spirit on Saul, already says:

> After that thou shalt come to the hill of God, where the garrison of the Philistines is: and when thou shalt be come there into the city, thou shalt meet a company of prophets coming down from the high place, with a psaltery and a timbrel, and a pipe, and a harp before them . . . And the spirit of the Lord shall come upon thee, and thou shalt prophesy with them, and shalt be changed into another man (1 Kings 10:5-6).

It will be later texts which lay emphasis on this point and throw still more light on the transforming action of the spirit of God.

2. POSSESSED BY THE SPIRIT

According to the Yahweh tradition, Balaam, before his third prophecy, was the first to be blessed with this "spirit of Yahweh."

> And lifting up his eyes, he saw Israel abiding in their tents by their tribes: and the spirit of God rushing upon him . . . (Num. 24:2).[3]

[3] This latter formula was long a classic (cf. 2 Par. 15:1; 20:14), but it was also said that the spirit "enveloped" the prophet, perhaps in the manner of military armor (Judges 6:34; 2 Par. 24:20), or that it "fell" upon him (Ezech. 11:5), or that it "lifted up" the prophet (Ezech. 3:12-14).

But writers of the Elohim tradition, with clearer insight had already told of Joseph, the interpreter of dreams, as a man possessed by the spirit of God:

> Can we find such another man, that is full of the spirit of God? (Gen. 41:38).[4]

A wholly special spirit had come upon Moses also, since God said to him, "I will take of thy spirit" to confer it upon the seventy men of the elders of Israel who shared with him a responsibility for the people (Num. 11:17). The elders then began to prophesy also, at least for that occasion:

> And the Lord came down in a cloud, and spoke to him, taking away of the spirit that was in Moses, and giving to the seventy men. And when the spirit had rested on them they prophesied . . . (Num. 11:25).

Let us note, in passing, that the action of the spirit is already more truly spiritual in these traditions. It no longer "swoops down" upon man, nor does it "compel" him, as in the time of the Judges, but more discreetly it "rests" upon the man who is chosen (we find the same conception in Is. 42:1). We should also bear in mind the idea of the transmission of the spirit, which we find in this passage.

[4] Daniel, presented in Joseph's image in the book which bears his name, is praised by Nabuchodonosor in identical terms: "[Daniel] who hath in him the spirit of the holy gods" (Dan. 4:5-6, 15; 11-12; 13:45). Daniel plays at Nabuchodonosor's court the role of an inspired Jew whose wisdom surpasses that of all the pagans, similar to that of Joseph with regard to the Egyptians and Pharaoh. It is the possession of the spirit which distinguishes the members of God's people from the pagans. Paul also put it well: "Whoever are led by the Spirit of God, they are the sons of God" (Rom. 8:14).

It will be found occurring again between Elias and Eliseus (4 Kings 2:15), and it is this transmission that best explains the rite of the laying on of hands, which the Church has sacramentalized with the same meaning and purpose.

Two men were absent from the camp during this first "Pentecost," but the spirit of God filled both of them, nevertheless. They began to prophesy in their turn. And Moses hoped that the same thing would happen to all of the people:

> O that all the people might prophesy, and that the Lord would give them his spirit! (Num. 11:29).

This hope and desire, doubtless influenced by Isaias 57:19 (see also Joel 2:28), was not fulfilled until the Pentecost of Acts 2:2-4, when the whole people received the Spirit of God.

Josue, who brought the work begun by Moses to a conclusion, was also a man in whom the spirit dwelled (Num. 27:18). Deuteronomy even connected this possession of the spirit by Josue with the laying on of hands conferred on him by the prophet (Deut. 34:9). Later, it was by the laying on of hands that the Apostles transmitted to new converts the Spirit which they had received on the day of the great Pentecost, foretold by the prophets.[5]

[5] Acts 8:17-24; 9:12-17. The Spirit is still transmitted in the Church during the sacraments of Confirmation and Holy Orders through the imposition of hands, just as in the early Church (cf. Acts 6:6; 13:1; 1 Tim. 4:14; 5:22). In the Acts, we note that the laying on of hands occurs when there are special missions entrusted to apostles.

Artisans responsible for making the tabernacle of God and objects for worship are described in the Book of Exodus (28:3) as endowed by God with the "spirit of wisdom."[6] One of them, Beseleel of Juda, we are told, was even filled with "the spirit of God, with wisdom and understanding, and knowledge in all manner of work" (Ex. 31:3; cf. 35:31). This passage already proclaims the spiritual riches that were later to be associated with Wisdom and follow upon possession of the Spirit of God in the sapiential books (Wisd. 7, 8; Is. 11:2).

3. FROM THE "POSSESSED" TO THE PROPHETS

It seems that "possession" by the spirit of God was for a long while considered with some reserve by the great prophets. Before the Exile we find hardly any prophets (except perhaps Micheas, in a difficult and doubtful text: Micheas 3:8; and Eliseus in 4 Kings 2:15), who regarded the *ruah* of such possession as the same prophetic spirit that characterized the earlier inspired men.

No doubt the rather "unspiritual" manifestations of this kind of prophesying account for their attitude. The prophetic spirit of these earlier "possessed" was too much like the human exaltation that accompanies enthusiasm, drunkenness, or anger, and its manifestations greatly resembled the unbridled agitation to which the false prophets of Baal lent themselves.

[6] The Jerusalem Bible translates this rather tritely as "exceptional ability."

After the Exile, however, Ezechiel no longer hesitated to say that he was "possessed" by the spirit, because of his nobler conception of the *ruah* of God.

This development again modified the ancient perspective, for the spirit of God was no longer the source of a somewhat unspiritual and momentary excitement, as with the "possessed," but it *remained* in the prophet whom it possessed. Heretofore, both heroes and zealots temporarily received this gift of the divine spirit. But now it remained in the man, always present in his ministry, preparing the way for the future conception of the indwelling of the Holy Spirit.

Ezechiel carried the idea of the spirit of God a step further when, no longer limiting the prophetic spirit to a spiritualization of respiratory breathing, he appealed additionally to the blast of the wind itself. Prophetic inspiration was not only the result of an interior action, but also the consequence of violent external activity, like that of the wind's. And thus we find once again the constant association of these two kinds or aspects of the "breath of God," determining the two phases of His activity: from within and from without.

> And the spirit took me up. . . . The Spirit also lifted me, and took me up. . . . between the earth and the heaven . . . (Ezech. 3:12, 14; 8:3).

> And the spirit lifted me up, and brought me into the east gate. . . . And the spirit lifted me up, and brought me into Chaldea. . . . The hand of the Lord was upon me, and brought me forth in the spirit of the Lord. . . . And the spirit lifted me up, and brought me into the inner court . . . (Ezech. 11:1, 24; 37:1; 43:5).

This spirit, however, also filled the prophet interiorly, as the prophetic spirit had penetrated the ancient prophets of earlier times. It "entered into him" like a new vital breath:

> And the spirit entered into me. . . . and he set me upon my feet: and I heard him speaking to me . . . (Ezech. 2:2; cf. also 1:4, 12, 20; 12:14; 13:13; 17:21).

Elsewhere, Ezechiel shows us the spirit of God coming down upon him in the way that the spirit of Yahweh suddenly descended on Saul (1 Kings 10:6-10).

In the older texts referring to Elias we already see the ancient prophet carried away by the spirit of Yahweh, thus escaping from all his enemies (3 Kings 18:12; 4 Kings 2:11-12, 16). Nearer our own time, the New Testament retained the imagery of prophetic inspiration as a wind that carries men off, and also as something inspired interiorly. The deacon Philip was taken away by the breath of God, the Spirit of the Lord (Acts 8:39) who, moreover, guided and counselled him (Acts 8:29).

This intervention of the wind, spiritualized as the "spirit of God," indicates a new aspect of prophesying, discovered and clarified by Ezechiel. The prophet's mission is not only a personal charism, but a communal function. The spirit is given for the community, and the prophet merely participates in the general gift in his particular way. By acting both interiorly and exteriorly, through the "new breath" and the "new wind," God reveals the two aspects of His own activity, and the spirit of the prophet is only a small part of the great wind of renewal transforming all the people. It is because of his awareness of the spirit's role in relation to the new people (cf. Ezech. 37) that Ezechiel also understood the spirit's role with regard to the prophet. We shall have occasion to consider further the communal dimension of the action of the spirit of God, as the successor to the "wind" of the Covenant and the Exodus (cf. Isaias 32:15, written later than Ezechiel).

4. THE MESSIAS KING

The gift of the spirit appears as a personal gift, but granted for the sake of the community. This gift of the spirit seems to be inseparable from some kind of mission (cf. Ezech. 11:24-25).

The mission may be prophetic or royal. It is not only the prophet whom the Bible regards as a man of the spirit. The consecration of David as king was accompanied by a descent of God's spirit upon him, and the anointing, performed by Samuel, appears in the sacred text as the source and cause of this descent. Today we would call this a sacrament.[7]

> Then Samuel took the horn of oil, and anointed him in the midst of his brethren: and the spirit of the Lord came upon David from that day forward . . . (1 Kings 16:13).

[7] It is true that David does not appear simply as a king but also as a prophet. Tradition would present him as a prophet (see 2 Kings 23:2, where the possession of the spirit and the "charism" of the word are placed side by side). Christians, inspired by the Spirit of God, participate in his anointing unto the threefold title of king, priest, and prophet, following Jesus, the head of the new inspired ones (cf. Is. 61:6; 1 Pet. 2:9-10; Apoc. 1:6; 5:10).

In the prophetic tradition, possession by the spirit remained as one of the characteristics of the Messias-king,[8] born of the house and succession of David, the son of Jesse:

> And there shall come forth a rod out of the root of Jesse, and a flower shall rise up out of his root. And the spirit of the Lord shall rest upon him: the spirit of wisdom, and of understanding, the spirit of counsel, and of fortitude, the spirit of knowledge, and of godliness (Is. 11:1-2).

This multiplication of names given to the spirit of Yahweh was meant to express all the wealth of spiritual gifts of which His spirit is the source. The many names have persisted. In the passage just quoted we find six characteristic names placed in apposition to the spirit of Yahweh. Later, in the Christian Church, and specifically in the rite of Confirmation, there will be the enumeration of the seven gifts of the Holy Spirit.[9]

In the prophecies of the Servant, there is mention of the spirit of God several times. The mysterious "Servant

[8] It will be noted, however, that 1 Kings 16:13 and 2 Kings 23:2 are relatively recent. It is not impossible that the primitive royalist traditions established no relationship between spirit and royalty, and that this relationship was only applied to David under the influence of Isaias' messianic theology.

[9] Compare, in Wisdom, all the spiritual riches whose sources are shown to be the spirit and wisdom, which work hand in hand (Wis. 7:7. Cf. Wis. 7:11; 7:22 fol.; 8:1-18). All of these developments regarding wisdom, the "spirit," and the riches of which they are the fount, are an amplification of 2 Paralipomenon 1:7-13, which is itself a reprise in different language of 3 Kings 3:5-15.

This text is the only one in the first part of the Book of Isaias (nevertheless, see Is. 4:4), in which the word "ruah" appears with the meaning of "spirit."

of Yahweh" is depicted as quite specially sustained and penetrated by the spirit:

> Behold my servant, I will uphold him: my elect, my soul delighteth in him: I have given my spirit upon him, and he shall bring forth judgment to the Gentiles. He shall not cry, nor have respect to person, neither shall his voice be heard abroad (Is. 42:1-2).[10]

> The spirit of the Lord is upon me, because the Lord hath anointed me: he hath sent me to preach to the meek, to heal the contrite of heart, and to preach a release to the captives, and deliverance to them that are shut up (Is. 61:1).[11]

Finally, the spirit was also given to judges and soldiers who collaborated in the establishment of the messianic era (Is. 28:6).

5. CONCLUSION

In breathing, man lives by the exhaling and inhaling of the "breath of God" in his nostrils. By devoting themselves to the service of God's purpose, heroes and chosen men lived by the coming-and-going of a breath of God, still transitory, which gave them power to fulfill this purpose. However, the action of this breath of God was purified, and thus truly deserved the change of name from "breath" to "spirit." It was no longer subject to the unpredictable coming and going of respiration or inspiration. Instead, it remained in the prophet, making a "new man" of him, capable of responding to God's plan

10 This text of Isaias will be quoted in Matthew 12:18.

11 This text of Isaias will be quoted in Luke 4:18.

and purpose for him in a prophetic or royal role. And although the breath of respiration was itself very different from the flesh that it animated, a fortiori the new breath transcended the world in which it was active, bringing about the fulfillment of a purpose conceived in the world of heaven.

It is striking to note that when the "breath of God" has been spiritualized and interiorized into the "spirit of God," it still retains its connection with that other "breath of God," the wind. We have already noted the importance accorded to the wind in prophetic inspiration, thus assuring the latter both cosmic and communal scope. God is forever active, both interiorly and exteriorly, through the individual and the community alike.

the Spirit and the Wind

As we pursue our study we shall note that the spirit of God, the spirit that was revealed by giving an increase of breath to the prophets and by sustaining them interiorly, will be mentioned more often than the breath or blast of the wind in all biblical descriptions of God's action upon the world. It will also appear as the source of a higher and more divine life than the life of which man's breath is the cause and sign. Nevertheless, the experience of the action of God's spirit upon mankind and the world will continue to be expressed in these more material terms.

Indeed, from one period to another, the prophets and wise men, forever meditating on the lessons of the past, express new ideas while using the same words and same imagery as the writers and inspired men who preceded them.

Consequently, we shall find frequent allusions to the wind and to the winds of God, or to the breath of life, in the writings of prophets, psalmists, and sages. These natural phenomena, which notably accompanied the miracle of the Passover, will now appear as traditional imagery intended to sustain and buttress the description of the spiritual action of God upon the people.

1. THE SPIRIT OF THE EXODUS

In the book of Isaias we find a poetic description of the Passover:

> I will remember the tender mercies of the Lord . . . so he became their savior. . . . and in his mercy he redeemed them, and he carried them and lifted them up all the days of old. But they provoked to wrath, and afflicted the spirit of his Holy One; and he was turned to be their enemy, and he fought against them. And he remembered the days of old of Moses, and of his people: where is he that brought them up out of the sea, with the shepherds of his flock? Where is he that put in the midst of them the spirit of his Holy One?[12] He that brought out Moses by the right hand, by the arm of his majesty: that divided the waters before them, to make himself an everlasting name. He that led them out through the deep, as a horse in the wilderness that stumbleth not. As a beast that goeth down in the field, the spirit of the

[12] Is. 63:11, to which must be added Ps. 2:13, are the only two passages in the Hebrew Old Testament in which the spirit is called "holy" (in the sense of *divine*). In Greek, however, the Septuagint version often added this adjective to the spirit of God, especially in the deutero-canonical books (Deut. 5:12; 6:4; Wis. 1:5; 7:22; 9:17). The subsequent revelation could not have been given better preparation.

> Lord was their leader: so didst thou lead thy people to make thyself a glorious name (Is. 63:7-19).
>
> O that thou wouldst rend the heavens, and wouldst come down: the mountains would melt away at thy presence (Is. 64:1).

In this text the remembrance of the wind that divided the waves of the Red Sea during the miracle of the ancient Passover, is still present. However, it cannot be said that "ruah elohim," as used in this instance, designates merely the wind of the Exodus, but rather the spirit of God intervening to save His people.

This is true of many poetic descriptions of the Passover and the people's trek through the desert. The remembrance of the wind that divided the sea and blew up a storm during the theophany of Sinai, is found in the theophanies related by the prophets (Ezech. 1:4, 12, 20-21; 10:17; Zach. 5:9). However, it was the spiritual action of God's spirit that was central in the thoughts of the psalmist, the prophet, or the sage.

In these descriptions, the action of the "wind of God" was not considered simply for its own sake. We see quite clearly that it was recalled especially because of its symbolism, and that it was mentioned to assure continuity between the interventions of God in behalf of His people through the elements of nature and those more spiritual interventions to which the prophets and psalmists were accustomed.

The Book of Nehemias (2 Esdras), of late composition, points out that God, during the Exile, gave His "good spirit" to the Hebrews (cf. Ps. 142:10, in which the psalmist asks God to lead him by His "good spirit"). According to Nehemias, the good spirit which God gives to men, and notably gave to the Hebrews during the Exodus and sojourn in the desert, appears almost as a participation in the spirituality of God Himself: "And thou gavest them thy good spirit" (2 Esd. 9:20).

At this stage, the "spirit of God" was already a term used in place of the name of God, in the same way as men spoke of His Holy Name, His Glory, or His Face. But "spirit" was distinctive inasmuch as it designated God according as He communicated Himself, and basically retained the connotation of a messenger of God's purpose.

2. THE SPIRIT AND WATER

By conserving the symbolism of the wind to signify the spiritual action of God over His people, the prophets kept and developed the connection long established by tradition between the wind and the rain of fertility.[13] This relation between the spirit and water even became one of the important prophetic themes after the Exile, thus serving as a prelude to Christian sacramentalism.

Accordingly, in the eyes of the prophets the pouring out of the spirit resembled the falling of the fertilizing rains brought by the wind to the desert:

> Until the spirit be poured upon us from on high: and the desert shall be as a charmel, and charmel shall be counted

[13] Cf. *supra*, p. 14.

> as a forest. And judgment shall dwell in the wilderness, and justice shall sit in charmel. And the work of justice shall be peace, and the service of justice quietness, and security forever. And my people shall sit in the beauty of peace, and in the tabernacles of confidence, and in wealthy rest (Is. 32:15-18).

> For I will pour out waters upon the thirsty ground, and streams upon the dry land: I will pour out my spirit upon thy seed, and my blessing upon thy stock. And they shall spring up among the herbs, as willows beside the running waters (Is. 44:3-4).[14]

The spirit of God was so often associated with the theme of fertility, as contrasted with the dry desert, that it was increasingly represented as water poured out. God "poured" His spirit upon the world (Ezech. 36:25-26; 39:29). Consequently, we see that it is not superfluous to note the verbs which express the action of God through His spirit. Whether these verbs indicate that the spirit was poured out upon man, or suddenly overwhelmed him, whether it rested on man or carried him away or descended gently upon him, each term includes a context that an attentive reader should not disregard.

Water, poured down in this way, fecundates the human desert and also purifies it:

> And I will pour upon you clean water, and you shall be cleansed from all your filthiness, and I will cleanse you from all your idols. And I will give you a new heart, and put a new spirit within you . . . (Ezech. 36:25-26).

14 To give these quotations their full meaning, it is necessary to recall that the miracle of the water gushing from the rock in the desert of Exodus (Ex. 17:5-6; Num. 20:7-11) is attributed to the spirit of God in the Judaic traditions.

This passage establishes a direct link between the water that cleanses and the spirit which is the source of new life. Only Christian Baptism, however, has completely fulfilled this text of Ezechiel. The theme of water is found earlier in Jeremias (31:9), as well as the theme of God as the source of life (Jer. 2:13; 17:13). But it was Ezechiel, the great prophet of the spirit of God, who was first to associate the spirit with this theme, by developing at a deeper level what the more ancient texts had already told us about the wind and water. After him, this association between the spirit of God and living water will appear frequently in the writings of the disciples of the prophet Isaias (Is. 32:15; 44:3; 4:4; 35:6-7; 43:20 and 55:1-10).

> . . . and now I will speak my judgments with them. Behold he shall come up as a cloud, and his chariots as a tempest: his horses are swifter than eagles . . . (Jer. 4:11-13).[15]

In Jewish literature there would always be the theme of the avenging wind, an instrument of God's judgment upon the unfaithful,[16] the inevitable concomitant of the last age and the Day of Yahweh. This brings us nearer the period when the last age would be called the Age of the Spirit. This is, however, only one episodic aspect of the general prophetic phenomenon which transposed the past occurrence of the ancient Exodus and its characteristics to the future.

[15] See also Jer. 13:24; 18:17; 22:22; 49:2.

[16] Image of the straw blown by the wind (Ps. 1:4; 34:5; 82:14); image of the judging of the nations by the wind (Ezech. 27:26).

4. CONCLUSION

Accordingly, it may be said that the revelation of the spirit of God continued to be identified with the characteristics of the wind's activity as the breath of God. Events of the past, in which the breath of God was manifested, were spiritualized when the prophets made of them the symbols of God's present and future action upon His people. From the wind that brings the fertilizing rain, to the spirit of God, considered as the source of living and purifying water, there is the whole distance between the material and the spiritual, but there is also a continuity between the symbol and reality. Whether under the breath of God or under the spirit of God, the same Exodus takes place and is celebrated, looking forward to the same Day of the Lord.

the Spirit and the New Man

The "ruah Elohim," prophetic or messianic inspiration rather than simple respiratory breath, became, in God's hands, the instrument used in creating a new Adam. The breath of Adam was weak and precarious, but the New Man, whether a prophet, messias, or one of the chosen few—and eventually the whole people would be prophetic, messianic, and chosen—now possessed more than animal breath. He was imbued with the authentic spirit of God.

When we analyze the characteristics of this spirit of God in man, we shall soon note that they are merely the sublimated characteristics of the ancient "breath of God." Here again the principle of continuity in regard to the theme becomes apparent.

1. THE LIFE-GIVING SPIRIT

The imagery of the breath that gives life is still present, but often sublimated, in the writings of the prophets and sages. However, it is no longer the respiratory breath animating natural life that is central in the prophet's thinking, but rather the spirit of God, that spirit which could restore life to the people of Israel who were considered as dead ever since the ordeal of exile had overwhelmed them.

Furthermore, the imagery of the wind and breath which engender or sustain life is often present whenever the prophets speak of the divine spirit.

We are familiar with the text of Ezechiel pertaining to the approaching resurrection of the people of God. The breath of God (which also intervenes as the manifestation of His spirit) had led the prophet into the plain where he received divine communications:

> The hand of the Lord was upon me, and brought me forth in the spirit of the Lord: and set me down in the midst of a plain that was full of bones. And he led me about through them on every side: now they were very many upon the face of the plain, and they were exceeding dry. And he said to me: Son of man, dost thou think these bones shall live? And I answered: O Lord God, thou knowest. And he said to me: Prophesy concerning these bones; and say to them: Ye dry bones, hear the word of the Lord.

> Thus saith the Lord God to these bones: Behold, I will send spirit into you, and you shall live. And I will lay sinews upon you, and will cause flesh to grow over you, and will cover you with skin: and I will give you spirit and you shall live, and you shall know that I am the Lord. And I prophesied as

> he had commanded me: and as I prophesied there was a noise, and behold a commotion: and the bones came together, each one to its joint.
>
> And I saw, and behold the sinews, and the flesh came up upon them: and the skin was stretched out over them, but there was no spirit in them. And he said to me: Prophesy to the spirit, prophesy, O son of man, and say to the spirit: Thus saith the Lord God: Come, spirit, from the four winds, and blow upon these slain, and let them live again. And I prophesied as he had commanded me: and the spirit came into them, and they lived: and they stood up upon their feet, an exceeding great army.
>
> And he said to me: Son of man: All these bones are the house of Israel: they say: Our bones are dried up, and our hope is lost, and we are cut off. Therefore prophesy, and say to them: Thus saith the Lord God: Behold I will open your graves, and will bring you out of your sepulchres, O my people: and will bring you into the Land of Israel. And you shall know that I am the Lord, when I shall have opened your sepulchres, and shall have brought you out of your graves, O my people: And shall have put my spirit in you, and you shall live, and I shall make you rest upon your own land: and you shall know that the Lord hath spoken, and done it, saith the Lord God (Ezech. 37:1-14).

It is nearly impossible in this passage to distinguish the occasions when "breath" or "spirit" should be understood as we read of "the wind," the "breath of life," or the "spirit of God."

Describing the miracle of resurrection (i.e. new creation) which took place before him, the prophet used for his own purposes the rather ingenuous but suggestive imagery of Genesis, in which life was communicated to the first man through the breath of the nostrils (Gen. 2:7), but he did this with unusual comprehensiveness. The same breath that entered into the dead bodies is the one that inspired his prophetic gift, and the same wind that carried him into the valley of dry bones was indeed the wind on whose wings God gave His own breath of life to His chosen people.

2. THE SPIRIT THAT CHANGES THE HEART

Ezechiel shows, however, that it is really a very different "breath" that matters now. A new breath will animate the people whom God will raise up, a breath which is no longer merely the sign and source of a natural life, but the necessary principle for living at a new level that is primarily moral, a level where God places the people resurrected by Himself. This new spirit, consequently, is no longer the breath that passes through the nostrils, but rather a spirit dwelling in the heart. According to Ezechiel, therefore, "to possess a new spirit," and "to possess a new heart," or "to create a new heart" or "a new spirit," are all synonymous. We know, of course, that the expression "a new heart," was already used in Jeremias (24:7; 32:40; cf. Deut. 30:6; Bar. 2:31), but it was Ezechiel who sufficiently refined the idea of breath to be able to make it synonymous with the idea of the heart (Ezech. 11:18-20; 18:31; cf. Ps. 50:12-13):

> And I will give them one heart, and will put a new spirit in their bowels: and I will take away the stony heart out of their flesh, and will give them a heart of flesh: That they may walk in my commandments, and keep my judgments, and do them . . . (Ezech. 11:19-20).

The "breath of God" had already appeared as expressing the thoughts and feelings of the heart: long-suffering, courage, astonishment, etc. But the spirit of God in the new man is notably more efficacious. It is at the very root of moral behavior, to such an extent that it is blended and identified with man's heart.

This means that a new covenant was sealed in which God no longer limits Himself to bringing an external law by the winds, or giving His people an external "breath" in order to obey it. Henceforth, the law is to be an interior gift, brought by the spirit of God Himself, and becomes both the source of the new law and grace to fulfill it. This points the way to the saying of St. Paul: "the letter kills, but the spirit gives life" (2 Cor. 3:6).

3. THE SPIRIT AND THE NEW COVENANT

As the spirit leads the people again into paradise, it also leads them into the Promised Land, "as a violent stream, which the spirit of the Lord driveth on" (Is. 59:19). It gives them again a law that is wholly interior, and seals the new covenant with them:

> And I will put my spirit in the midst of you: and I will cause you to walk in my commandments, and to keep my judgments, and do them. And you shall dwell in the land which I gave to your fathers, and you shall be my people, and I will be your God (Ezech. 36:27-28).

> And they shall know that I am the Lord their God, because I caused them to be carried away among the nations; and I have gathered them together unto their own land, and

> have not left any of them there. And I will hide my face no more from them, for I have poured out my spirit upon all the house of Israel, saith the Lord God (Ezech. 39:28-29).

> And you shall know that I am the Lord . . . and shall have put my spirit in you, and you shall live, and I shall make you rest upon your own land: and you shall know that I the Lord have spoken . . . (Ezech. 37:14; cf. Is. 61:1-4).

These texts of Ezechiel repeat, word for word, several expressions of Exodus that can be found earlier in Deuteronomy, transposed into a new language and spirit.

> This is my covenant with them, saith the Lord: My spirit that is in thee, and my words that I have put in thy mouth, shall not depart out of thy mouth, nor out of the mouth of thy seed, nor out of the mouth of thy seed's seed, saith the Lord, from henceforth and for ever (Is. 59:21).

Consequently, the spirit of God, in the new spiritual structure which was being developed, would function as the breath of God, bringing new life, as the source of interior virtues and graces, the primordial basis of the new covenant.

However, this structure was still in gestation. The spirit of God, presiding over this evolution and informing it, would itself give way to a still greater power: the Holy Spirit of the Father, at long last bringing forth in splendor the perfection of His work and the fulfillment of its spiritualization.

4. THE SPIRIT AND WISDOM

Even when it became the principle of moral life and the new covenant, the spirit of God in the heart of the elect often kept an intellectual aspect. It was a counsellor to be questioned, and at the same time a life-giving power. The wise men of Israel, who laid claim to the prophetic heritage of the spirit (cf. Ecclus. 39:8; Wisd. 7:7; 9:17), rapidly began identifying the spirit with wisdom[17] by laying stress upon the first of these two aspects of the spirit.

The spirit of God continued to be the fundamental element of the new covenant, but its role as counsellor and teacher was emphasized:

> For the Holy Spirit of discipline will flee from the deceitful, and will withdraw himself from thoughts that are without understanding, and he shall not abide when iniquity cometh in (Wisd. 1:5).

Under this educative aspect, the spirit of God was often called the "good spirit" (Ps. 142:10; 2 Esd. 9:20), who guided and governed with prudence.

[17] Cf. Wis. 1:4-6; 7:22-24; 9:17.

Conclusion: the Renewal in the Last Age

From the period of the wisdom writers, the messianic time was described as the age of the outpouring of the spirit, and the prophecy of Isaias was not without echo:

> This is my covenant with them, saith the Lord: My spirit that is in thee, and my words that I have put in thy mouth, shall not depart out of thy mouth, nor out of the mouth of thy seed, nor out of the mouth of thy seed's seed, saith the Lord, from henceforth and for ever (Is. 59:21).

There is a great distance between this spirit of God, as mentioned by the prophets, and the wind of God that divided the Red Sea (Ex. 14:21), a wind which, roaring around Mount Sinai, brought quails and manna to the people during their journey across the desert. This breath of Yahweh also appears as something quite different from the breath of respiration or the panting breath of the prophets of old.

It was the spirit of God, and no longer the wind, which was the source and cause of the new people of God who would be born after the great ordeal. It was the spirit of God, and no longer the breath of respiration, which indwelled and would always indwell the renewed hearts of men in their new covenant with God. It was the spirit of God, and no longer merely a prophetic spirit, that rested, and would always rest upon the servant of God, called to lead the people whom God had chosen.

However, all the ancient meanings of the word "ruah" formed the background for the thinking of the biblical writers. The action of God's spirit resembled that of the wind that divides the sea, or the breath that sustains life, or the breath that inspired the "possessed" long centuries before.

All that God accomplished or would yet achieve, and all that He proclaimed through the mouth of His prophets, seemed indeed to be a reminder of what God had formerly accomplished for the salvation of His people. The action of the spirit of God thus seems to have been closely connected with the remembrance of the desert, the place of the first teaching of the people by God Himself.

The future stage of salvation over which the spirit of God would preside, consequently tended toward final fulfillment of whatever had merely been outlined or vaguely prefigured in the past. The people would seal a new covenant with God and enter into a land of milk and honey, recovering Jerusalem again, their capital, while also receiving the communication of a principle of new life, far above the principle of natural life, which would cleanse them of their faults and lift them to the level required by their new state of life, and all of this would take place through the action of the spirit of God.

The spirit thus seems to be bound up with the last age, with the mission of ensuring its complete fulfillment.

In that age, however, being fulfilled with the spirit would no longer be the prerogative of a few inspired men, responsible for leading the people. The spirit would be given in such abundance that every member of the community would in some way be inspired and would prophesy:

> And it shall come to pass after this, that I will pour out my spirit upon all flesh: and your sons and your daughters shall prophesy: your old men shall dream dreams, and your young men shall see visions.
>
> Moreover, upon my servants and handmaids in those days I will pour forth my spirit . . .
>
> And it shall come to pass that everyone that shall call upon the name of the Lord shall be saved: for in mount Sion, and in Jerusalem, shall be salvation, as the Lord hath said, and in the residue whom the Lord shall call (Joel 2:28-29, 32).

The spirit of God, moreover, was already dwelling in the midst of the saved who had established themselves in Palestine after the marvellous return from exile (Agg.

2:5; cf. Zach. 6:8). The spirit rested upon those men, like Zorobabel, who presided over the reconstruction of the city and the Temple. It was from the spirit that all their power and strength were derived (Zach. 4:6). From this time on, pious Jews, hearing mention of the spirit of God, knew that the spirit was the supernatural power that would some day burst forth in eruption, breaking asunder the very structure of the whole world, purifying its faults and flaws, and fecundating its sterility. They looked to this same supernatural power to ensure the establishment between God and men of a new covenant, definitive and all-embracing, and to make a new paradise of the universe which it had saved. All men would then have a new heart, for the spirit, as in the past, would act not only in an external and overwhelming manner, but also discreetly, deep in the minds and hearts of men.[18]

Only Pentecost and the full outpouring of the spirit in the last days could now fulfill the expectation of pious Jews. And on the day of the divine spirit's coming would be revealed, even more wonderfully, the divine personality of the Holy Spirit.

[18] Joel 3:1; Is. 32:15; 34:16; Ezech. 11:19; 36:26-27; 37:4-14.

Chapter Three

THE HOLY SPIRIT

Pious Jews, taught by meditation on Scripture and their personal contact with the spirit, all lived in expectation of the fulfillment of Joel's glorious prophecy. The times of tribulation which were endured "in the days of king Herod" (Luke 1:5) made them long ardently for the coming of the spirit for the "redemption of Jerusalem" (cf. Luke 2:38).

Indeed, Pentecost not only fulfilled, but even far surpassed their expectation. It was not simply the spirit, but indeed the *Holy Spirit* who came to fill the whole world and to create a new universe.

This Holy Spirit, a personal Being, suddenly came forth as "a powerful wind," driving the Apostles out into all the world, and as a breath of life, engendering and sustaining the Church. He appeared as a prophetic spirit inspiring the disciples of Jesus, the new prophets of the Lord, after His resurrecting of the Christ, the new Adam.

A

the New Pentecost

1. THE SPIRIT IN THE NEW TESTAMENT

The Greek word "pneuma" (*πνευμα*)—which corresponds almost exactly to the Hebrew "ruah" in the Greek translation of the Bible, called the Septuagint—is often used in the writings of the New Testament. We find it again and again with all the meanings encountered with regard to "ruah" in the Old Testament: the breath of respiration,[1] the breath of life,[2] the blowing wind,[3] mind and soul,[4]

[1] In general, however, the New Testament uses the word "psuchê" (ψυχή), which designates simultaneously the breath of respiration and life itself. We shall see that it is not by accident that John, speaking of the death of Our Lord, says that Jesus "gave up the Spirit" and not "gave up His soul."

[2] Luke 8:55; Apoc. 11:11; 13:15.

[3] John 3:8; Heb. 1:7.

[4] Mark 2:8.

moral disposition,[5] good or evil spirit.[6] It is used primarily, however, to designate the spirit of God, or rather the Holy Spirit, a divine Person who fully revealed Himself to the Twelve after the glorification of Jesus.

The word "spirit" sometimes appears without the adjective "holy," particularly in the Gospels, and most noticeably in Matthew, but generally the writings of the New Testament make reference to "the Holy Spirit," although there is no importance to be attributed either to the presence or the absence of the adjective. We may, for instance, compare Matthew 12:31, Luke 2:27 and Acts 2:4, where we find that the term is used both with and without the adjective. Occasionally, within parallel passages, mention is made of "the Spirit" and "the Holy Spirit."[7]

By studying some of the more important passages of the New Testament regarding the Holy Spirit, we shall note the progressive character of the revelation of the Spirit, so clearly attested by the texts of the New Testament, and at the same time see that a real continuity is maintained. It is indeed the same spirit that is revealed to us, but now in a close and intimate communion between human persons and a divine Person.

[5] Matt. 5:3; 1 Pet. 3:4.

[6] Matt. 8:16; 10:1; Acts 8:7; Eph. 2:2.

[7] Matt. 3:16 and Mark 1:10, as against Luke 3:22 and John 1:32; Matt. 22:43 as against Mark 12:36.

2. PENTECOST

On the morning of Pentecost, the disciples of Jesus were gathered together. Jesus was present among them:

> And while eating with them, he charged them not to depart from Jerusalem, but to wait for the promise of the Father, "of which you have heard," said he, "by my mouth; for John indeed baptized with water, but you shall be baptized with the Holy Spirit not many days hence" (Acts 1:4-5).

For ten days they continued in prayer, all of them imbued with the same desire (Acts 1:14). No doubt Mary, the mother of Jesus, was among them. The Holy Spirit was coming, like a breath of life, to create the Church.

The disciples, as devout Jews, were celebrating the Feast of Weeks together.[8] Although they were not aware of it they were already fulfilling Joel's prophecy:

> And it shall come to pass, that everyone that shall call upon the name of the Lord shall be saved: for in Mount Sion and in Jerusalem shall be salvation . . . (Joel 11:32).

Certainly they were overwhelmed by the events they had just experienced, and by the teachings of their Master, and doubtless they anticipated some kind of immediate fulfillment:

> . . . but you shall be baptized with the Holy Spirit not many days hence (Acts 1:5).

"Baptized" did not have a sacramental connotation in this context. The word means "to immerse" and pertains to

[8] Acts 2:1; cf. Ex. 23:16; Lev. 23:15; Deut. 16:9.

the vocabulary of water, like the verb "to pour" which we have seen used interchangeably in reference to water or the spirit.[9]

The Holy Spirit, wonderfully promised by the Father, would now appear, bringing with Him the restoration of paradise and Jerusalem, and achieve the redemption of Israel.

Pentecost, which the Apostles were then celebrating, brought an end to the paschal feasts, but these had been feasts that began for them in great trouble and sorrow. For the Jews, Pentecost was a special remembrance of the promulgation of the Law on Sinai and the sealing of the Covenant.

Later traditions taught that the theophany of Sinai had taken place fifty days after the crossing of the Red Sea.

And now, suddenly, both wind and fire appeared as long ago on Sinai (Ex. 19:16), when God spoke with Moses. The expectation of the apostles was fulfilled; the past was re-enacted at a deeper level:

> And suddenly there came a sound from heaven, as of a violent wind blowing, and it filled the whole house where they were sitting. And there appeared to them parted tongues as of fire, which settled upon each of them. And they were all filled with the Holy Spirit and began to speak in foreign tongues, even as the Holy Spirit prompted them to speak (Acts 2:2-4).

9 Cf. *supra*, p. 78. The term "pour forth" will, moreover, continue to be frequent in the vocabulary of the New Testament, thanks to the influence of Joel 3:1-2; cf. Acts 2:17-18; 33; 10:45; Rom. 5:5; Tit. 3:6.

The study that we have been pursuing in these pages gives a real meaning to all the elements of the description in this passage from Acts. The Spirit of God is manifested in the wind, since there is a "blowing" as of air in motion; and because the prophets are impelled to speak.[10] The Spirit is also manifested in the form of tongues, in this instance burning tongues, since it was in the form of a burning bush and fire that God had revealed Himself to Moses and to Abraham, long before.[11]

3. THE FULFILLMENT OF JOEL'S PROPHECY

Peter, the chief Apostle, speaking in the name of all the Apostles and disciples, found no difficulty in explaining to the assembled people all that was happening. The prophet Joel's words came immediately to his mind and lips. There were "wonders in the heavens" just as Joel had prophesied when he spoke of the last age (Joel 3:3-4, cf. Acts 2:19-20; Joel 3:1-21, cf. Acts 2:17-18 and 39).

The Holy Spirit was poured out upon "His servants and handmaids," who began to prophesy. Soon He would be poured out upon "all flesh," and that is what happened one day in Jerusalem when men of all nations and peoples

[10] On the link between Word and Spirit, cf. Num. 11:1, 25; 1 Kings 10:5-6; 16:13; 19:20-24; 3 Kings 22:10.

[11] Ex. 3:2; cf. Gen. 15:17; Ex. 19:18; 24:17; Deut. 4:12, 24; 9:3; Ps. 49:3. Jesus was unquestionably referring to the Spirit when He said that He had come to cast fire upon the earth (Luke 12:49; cf. 3:16).

had gathered there (Acts 2:5-11). Moses' desire to see the spirit of God rest upon not only a few who were specially chosen, but on all the people (Num. 11:29) was at last fulfilled.[12] The last age, the new times foretold by the prophets, had arrived.

With extraordinary enthusiasm, and even somewhat ingenuously, the primitive community of Jerusalem felt that they were living over again the experience of the Chosen People, carried forward by the Spirit of God toward fulfillment of their calling. Miracles were occurring at every turn (Acts 2:43; 4:30; 5:12, etc.). The Spirit of God manifested His power in a special manner by the driving out of evil spirits (Acts 5:16; 8:17).

The gathering of the community that took place following Peter's arrest and release, was the occasion of another series of miracles (Acts 4:31). An earthquake seemed to shake the room in which the disciples were assembled, as if once again the elements of earth could not stand fast in the presence of the heavenly element that had just irrupted, all of this happening as it had in ancient times when the Spirit was poured out upon men:

> And when they had prayed, the place where they had assembled was shaken, and they were all filled with the Holy Spirit, and spoke the word of God with boldness (Acts 4:31).

12 The "promise of the Father" (Acts 1:4; 2:33, 39; 13:32; 26:6) is indeed valid for the entire universe "for all flesh" (Joel 3:1; Is. 2:2-4; 49:1; 66:19; Acts 2:39). The Acts explicitly connect this promise of the Spirit to that made to Abraham for all nations (Acts 3:25; 7:17). Acts also recalls the promises of Isaias quoted above (Acts 15:13-14).

Possession by the new spirit was quite as contagious as possession by the prophetic spirit that filled the ancient inspired men of the remote past.[13]

4. A DIVINE PERSON

The Apostles lived so intimately with the Spirit that it seemed as though He was a part of their community, one of their members, a real person living among themselves:

> And we are witnesses of these things, and so is the Holy Spirit, whom God has given to all who obey him (Acts 5:32).

These were the words of Peter when he was brought before the Sanhedrin the second time.

After the Council of Jerusalem, the Apostles expressed their oneness with the Spirit clearly and emphatically:

> For the Holy Spirit and we have decided to lay no further burden upon you but this indispensable one . . . (Acts 15:28).

The Spirit was so completely a part of the new community that any harm done to the community was somehow an act against the Holy Spirit (Acts 5:3-9; 7:51).

5. CONCLUSION: THE SPIRIT IN THE PREACHING OF THE APOSTLES

The Holy Spirit was accorded a place of pre-eminence in the preaching of the Apostles. They proclaimed to the

[13] Acts 2:47, which refers implicitly to Joel 3:5; compare 1 Kings 10:5-6; 19:23-24.

whole world that it was the Spirit who had been given to them, and that He was now offered to all men, regardless of race, for their salvation, through the grace of Jesus whom God had glorified. Moreover, they soon associated the universal gift of the Spirit with the promise made to Abraham, extending to all the families of the earth (Gen. 12:3, 22:18; cf. Acts 3:25; Gal. 3:8-29; Rom. 15:8).

In their hearts there was the constant echo of the prophetic promise made by God to Joel and proclaimed by this prophet to all who lived in expectation of the last days, a prophecy and promise which the Apostles had seen fulfilled (Joel 2:28-32).

They spoke of the Spirit as the real object of the promise, a gift of God surpassing all else (Acts 2:38; cf. Luke 11:13). They recalled the prophecies and promises of the Old Testament at the same time as they made special reference to the promise of the Father at the moment when John the Baptist was sent into the wilderness, a promise renewed by Jesus before His ascension:

> . . . for John indeed baptized with water, but you shall be baptized with the Holy Spirit not many days hence . . . (Acts 1:5; cf. 11:16).

They proclaimed that the Spirit was now offered to all mankind (Acts 2:17; cf. Joel 3:1), whereas formerly the pouring forth of the Spirit had been restricted to a chosen few. Finally, the Apostles taught that the Spirit was offered for man's salvation (Acts 2:38-39; cf. Is. 57:19; Joel 3:5).

They explained how and why the Spirit could now be given and offered to all men everywhere, as the consequence of the glorification of Jesus. It was following His passion, resurrection and ascension into Heaven that He was fully recognized as the Christ, "the Anointed of God," and was revered as the Lord (Acts 2:36).

This outpouring of the Spirit was actually occurring. It had already begun and would continue thereafter. In itself it was the proof, clearly available to everyone, that Jesus, who had been crucified, and whose body had undergone no decay in the tomb, was indeed Christ and Lord:

> "Men of Judea and all you who dwell in Jerusalem, says the Lord, let this be known to you, and give ear to my words . . . this is what was spoken through the prophet Joel:
>
> *And it shall come to pass in the last days, says the Lord, that I will pour forth of my Spirit upon all flesh . . .*
>
> Men of Israel, hear these words. Jesus of Nazareth was a man approved by God among you by miracles and wonders and signs, which God did through him in the midst of you, as you yourselves know. Him, when delivered up by the settled purpose and foreknowledge of God, you have crucified and slain by the hands of wicked men. But God has raised him up. . . . and we are all witnesses of it. Therefore, exalted by the right hand of God, and receiving from the Father the promise of the Holy Spirit, he has poured forth this Spirit which you see and hear. . . . Repent and be baptized everyone of you in the name of Jesus Christ for the forgiveness of your sins; *and you will receive the gift of the Holy Spirit. For to you is the promise* and to your children and to all who are far off, even to all whom the Lord our God calls to himself . . ." (Acts 2:14-39).

It is the role of the Spirit to transform all those who are indwelled by Himself into witnesses of Christ, who rose from the dead (Acts 1:8), thus making them prophets of the Lord (Acts 2:17-18; cf. Joel 3:1-2). All whom the Spirit touches, and who are impelled by Him, become prophets of the resurrection of Christ through a whole new life[14] which implies, as we shall soon see, a participation in the spiritual resurrection of the Lord.

Peter declared, moreover, that a man must prepare himself for the gift of the Spirit by conversion, baptism, and separation from the world of men (Acts 2:38-40).

In the preaching of the Apostles, this spirit of Pentecost and of salvation was described as "the gift" and the "promise of the Father." They also spoke of the "Spirit of Jesus," for the glorified Jesus possesses this holy spirit to be transmitted to all mankind.

In their exact meaning, the terms used in Peter's first sermon would seem to suggest that Jesus did not possess the Spirit, and was not Christ and Lord, until after His glorification, considered as recompense for His humiliation and the sufferings of His passion.[15]

It was not long until the basis and reference of the initial preaching of the Apostles, exclusively centered upon the paschal mystery of Christ's glorification, was

14 Cf. *Cahier "Evangile,"* no. 12: *L'Eglise naît,* pp. 27 ff.

15 The letters addressed by Paul to the Romans and to Titus also bring us the echo of this initial view of the early Church regarding the mystery of Jesus. Paul seems to be quoting there (Rom. 1:2-3; Tit. 3:16) two fragments of hymns in use in the early Church during the first Christian liturgical celebrations.

considerably enlarged (cf. Acts 10:34-48). But it seemed appropriate to take note of this before studying what the letters of the Apostles may teach us about the Spirit.

The whole mystery of the glorified Jesus, pouring forth the Spirit for the salvation of mankind, was attested by the Apostles, together with the Holy Spirit Himself, who witnessed with them:

> The God of our fathers raised Jesus, whom you put to death, hanging him on a tree. Him God exalted with his right hand to be Prince and Savior, to grant repentance to Israel and forgiveness of sins. And we are witnesses of these things, and so is the Holy Spirit, whom God has given to all who obey him (Acts 5:30-32).

B

the New Prophets

As the breath of God inspired the "heroes" in the first days of the Chosen People, and as the spirit of God filled the prophets of the new covenant, similarly the Holy Spirit, from the moment of His appearance, formed a nucleus of servants for tasks of a special kind.

1. THE PROPHET

All the members of the new community appear as men moved by the Spirit who inspired them even more constantly than the most favored of the inspired men of old. He impelled them like a wind, and gave them a new life. He transformed them into witnesses for God, and made prophets of them all.

Peter, the chief of the Apostles, who had once been so timid, but was now filled with the Holy Spirit, spoke boldly before the Sanhedrin (Acts 4:8). Taken into custody after healing the lame man at the Beautiful Gate, Peter used the occasion to proclaim Jesus as the Savior of men.[16]

In obedience to the Spirit, Peter set out for Caesarea, following his vision at Jaffa (Acts 10:17-19; 11:12). It was the Holy Spirit who explained the vision's meaning to him.

Barnabas and his companions, the "prophets and priests" of the first little church at Antioch, also lived in constant touch with the Holy Spirit (Acts 11:24). He spoke to them, and it was in obedience to Him that they pursued their mission:

> And as they were ministering to the Lord and fasting, the Holy Spirit said, "Set apart for me Saul and Barnabas unto the work to which I have called them" (Acts 13:2).

The Book of Acts shows us in a remarkably full way the role of the Spirit in the guidance of Paul, the convert of Damascus. At the time of the visit of Ananias and of Paul's baptism, the Spirit had already "filled"[17] Paul and made another man of him (Acts 9:17-19; cf. Acts 22:19; 26:29. Cf. 1 Kings 10:5-6).

It was under the guidance of the Spirit that Paul made his journey to Jerusalem (Acts 20:22), and that he

[16] Acts 4:8-12; cf. Matt. 10:17-20; Acts 5:32.

[17] A new formula to describe the action of the Spirit; Luke is particularly fond of it, no doubt because it is a good expression of the actual fulness: cf. Luke 1:15; 41, 67; Acts 2:4; 4:8, 31; 9:17; 13:9. This formula is all the more apt in that it clearly indicates the context of "fulness" in which the Holy Spirit operates. It suffices to compare it with the formulas of the Old Testament.

travelled with Barnabas to Seleucia, and then to Cyprus (Acts 13:4).

During his second journey, the Spirit had forbidden Paul to preach the word in Asia or in Bithynia (Acts 16:6-7). Later, he said that he was "compelled by the Spirit" (literally "bound" or chained) to go up to Jerusalem (Acts 20:22).

Stephen, even more than his companions, the first deacons (Acts 6:3), was a man filled with the Holy Spirit (Acts 6:5). The great sin that he condemned in his accusers, the Greek-speaking Jews, together with all the members of the Sanhedrin, was their constant resistance to the Holy Spirit.[18] As they were all gnashing their teeth at him, Stephen, being full of the Holy Spirit, beheld "the glory of God, and Jesus standing at the right hand of God" (Acts 7:55).

The Book of Acts shows us Philip, running, as the Spirit had commanded him, to overtake the carriage of the minister of Candace, the Queen of Ethiopia:

> And the Spirit said to Philip, "Go near and keep close to this carriage" (Acts 8:29).

And then he was somehow taken away by the Spirit of the Lord as soon as he had baptized the queen's minister, almost in the manner of Elias and Ezechiel:

> But when they came up out of the water, the Spirit of the Lord took Philip away, and the eunuch saw him no more. . . . But Philip was found in Azotus . . . (Acts 8:39).

[18] Acts 7:51; cf. Num. 27:14; Is. 63:10; Acts 5:1-11.

Among the prophets who had a special role in the primitive Church,[19] we must take note of Agabus who rose up one day in the church at Antioch and revealed "through the Spirit" that there would be a great famine all over the world. It was then that Barnabas and Paul were sent to help the church in Jerusalem (Acts 11:27-30). It was this same prophet, Agabus, who later foretold Paul's impending arrest:

> And while we were staying on there for some days, there came down from Judea a certain prophet named Agabus. Coming to us, and taking Paul's girdle, he bound his own feet and hands, and said, "Thus says the Holy Spirit: The man whose girdle this is, the Jews will bind like this at Jerusalem, and they will deliver him into the hands of the Gentiles" (Acts 21:10-11).

Agabus, inspired by the Holy Spirit, acted in this instance like the ancient prophets of Israel when, inspired by the divine breath, they performed a symbolic act and then explained its meaning, as they proclaimed in God's name the prophecy which He had placed upon their lips.[20]

2. THE WITNESS

a) *Witnessing and the Spirit*

Like the breath of God in earlier times, the gift of the Spirit, a personal gift, seemed to be connected with either

[19] Acts 13:1; 15:32; 19:6; 21:9-10; 1 Cor. 12:28-30; 14:1-40; Eph. 4:11.

[20] 3 Kings 11:29-39; 20:35-43; Os. 1:2; 3:1-5; Is. 20:1-6; Jer. 13:1-11; 19:1; 27:1; Ezech. 3:22-27; 4:1-17; 12:1-10; 24:1-27.

the particular mission of the ministry, or with the general mission of witnessing, which pertains to all Christians and, a fortiori, to the Apostles:

> . . . you shall receive power when the Holy Spirit comes upon you, and you shall be witnesses for me in Jerusalem and in all Judea and Samaria and even to the very ends of the earth (Acts 1:8).[21]

Analysis of this apostolic witnessing soon shows that it was closely connected with the prophetic function of the Old Covenant. The same spirit inspired the two activities, and the two outstanding witnesses of the Apocalypse were both prophets and apostles:[22]

> And I will grant unto my two witnesses to prophesy for a thousand two hundred and sixty days, clothed in sackcloth (Apoc. 11:3).

The prophetic function and that of witnessing were so closely related, moreover, that the prophets, in their turn, were called "witnesses":

> To him all the prophets bear witness, that through his name all who believe in him may receive forgiveness of sins (Acts 10:43).[23]

[21] Cf. Acts 1:22; 2:32; 3:15; 4:33; 5:32; 10:39-41; 13:31. Regarding the contents of the testimony in Acts, cf. Cerfaux, "Témoins du Christ," *Recueil Cerfaux,* II, 153-174; Rétif, "Témoignage et prédication missionnaire," *N. R. Th.,* 1951, 152-165.

[22] John indeed describes the activity and the martyrdom of Peter and Paul in light of the characteristics of these two "prophets."

[23] Cf. also Acts 26:22 and, for the Old Testament, Is. 63:7.

The angel of revelation could tell John, in the same sense, that the witnessing of Jesus was the spirit of prophecy.[24]

The only difference between the prophet and the witness is found in the fact that the former announces the event, whereas the latter declares its occurrence and fulfillment. To be a witness of the Resurrection is to show by word and deed that God's design and purpose were fulfilled in that event. And if the "witnesses of the Resurrection" had recourse so readily to prophetic texts to justify the fact of the Resurrection, it must not be supposed that this was merely an apologetical procedure making use of the scriptural evidence.

In reality, the witness thus affirms the continuity of his mission with regard to the mission of the prophets, under the influence of the Spirit who witnesses through both (Acts 5:32). This was especially well expressed by Peter:

> To them [the prophets] it was revealed that not to themselves but to you they were ministering those things which now have been declared to you by those who preached the gospel to you by the Holy Spirit sent from heaven (1 Pet. 1:12).

The witness is therefore the central figure in the economy of the "last days," when everything is fulfilled. He is the legitimate successor of the prophet, the central figure of a dispensation that is still evolving and expectant.

24 Cf. Apoc. 1:2, 9; 12:17; 19:10; 20:4.

b) *Martyrdom and the Spirit*[25]

The witness does not only proclaim the fact of an historical event; the event engages and involves his life, compelling him to make a choice. It is not surprising that this witnessing often culminates in the need to testify before human judges and persecutors:

> And when they have finished their testimony, the beast that comes up out of the abyss will wage war against them, and will conquer them and will kill them (Apoc. 11:7).

Moreover, Christ had foreseen that the testimony of His followers would lead to the witnessing of martyrdom:

> . . . they will arrest you and persecute you, delivering you up to the synagogues and prisons, dragging you before kings and governors for my name's sake. It shall lead to your bearing witness (Luke 21:12-13).[26]

In witness which reaches the point of martyrdom the Holy Spirit appears again, inspiring the martyrs as He inspired the prophets. In a text similar to the one just quoted, Christ counsels future witnesses:

> And when they bring you before the synagogues and the magistrates and the authorities, do not be anxious how or wherewith you shall defend yourselves, or what you shall say, for the Holy Spirit will teach you in that very hour what you ought to say (Luke 12:11-12).

[25] Let us recall that μαρτυρ, "martyr," is the same Greek word that also means witness. It has entered our language to designate the testimony par excellence, the testimony of blood. In the terminology of the New Testament, it covers, along with the testimony of the word, that of the works accomplished by the Apostles, and the mutual love they had for one another and even for those who would hate them without reason.

[26] Translation suggested by Cerfaux, *op. cit.*, p. 168. Cf. also John 16:2.

Indeed, in his appearance before the Sanhedrin, Peter was "filled with the Holy Spirit" (Acts 4:8). And Stephen, in the presence of his accusers, appeared transfigured by the Spirit whom they could not withstand (Acts 6:10; 7:51). The martyred witnesses of the Apocalypse would likewise receive the life-giving help of the Spirit in the way that Adam received the Spirit's breath:

> And after the three days and a half, the breath of God entered into them. And they stood up on their feet . . . (Apoc. 11:11).[27]

John, confronting the problem of the first heresies, did not hesitate to regard witnessing and the "confession" of God's name as the essential criterion of the presence of the Spirit of God:

> By this is the spirit of God known: every spirit that confesses that Jesus Christ has come in the flesh, is of God. And every spirit that severs Jesus, is not of God, but is of Antichrist (1 John 4:2-3).

The first liberating heroes of the people needed a special breath in their lungs to achieve the tremendous task of liberation. The prophets needed the very spirit of God to reveal the Father's plan and purpose for mankind. But only the Holy Spirit can transform a man into a witness and martyr.

c) *The great witness: the Paraclete*

Already in the Book of Acts, the witnessing and martyrdom of witnesses was eclipsed by the witnessing

[27] Recalls also the vision in Ezech. 37.

of the Holy Spirit Himself (Acts 5:32; Luke 12:12), which John mentioned in his first epistle.

> Who is there that overcomes the world if not he who believes that Jesus is the Son of God? This is he who came in water and in blood, Jesus Christ; not in the water only, but in the water and in the blood. And it is the Spirit that bears witness that Christ is the truth. For there are three that bear witness in heaven: the Father, the Word, and the Holy Spirit; and these three are one. And there are three that bear witness on earth: the Spirit, and the water, and the blood; and these three are one. If we receive the testimony of men, the testimony of God is greater; for this is the testimony of God which is greater, that he has borne witness concerning his Son. He who believes in the Son of God has the testimony of God in himself (1 John 5:5-10).

However, John developed this theology of the Spirit's witnessing even further by pointing out, in the discourse following the Last Supper, the role of the "Paraclete" which was undertaken by the Spirit after the Lord's departure (John 14:15-17, 25-26; 15:26-27; 16:7-14).[28]

As an all-powerful advocate, a Paraclete defends the case of anyone who is likely to be condemned before a tribunal (cf. 1 John 2:1), or he seeks to appeal an unjust sentence. He also brings help and assistance to those who are in need, not only by his counselling but with the full support of his authority and power.

The word "Paraclete" occurs rarely in the New Testament,[29] but the similar term, "paraclesis," is frequent.

[28] Cf. A. Lemonnyer, "L'Esprit Saint Paraclet," *R. Sc. Ph. Th.*, 1927, 293-317; Berrouard, "Le Paraclet, défenseur du Christ," *ibid.*, 1948, 361-389.

[29] Four times in the discourse after the Last Supper and once in 1 John 2:1. It never appears in the Old Testament, except in the Symmachus and Theodotion versions of Job 16:2. Even so, the meaning of the word here (comforter) is not that of John.

Paraclesis is the special function of the Holy Spirit, and one of the essential functions of the apostle, His witness. The paraclesis of the Holy Spirit is clearly described for us in the Book of Acts:

> Now throughout all Judea and Galilee and Samaria the Church was in peace and was being built up, walking in fear of the Lord, and it was filled with the consolation of the Holy Spirit (Acts 9:31).

It was indeed all of this assistance that our Lord promised to His apostles in His last discourse (John 14:1-16). This assistance was to develop, in one respect, at a certain juridical level, with the Holy Spirit victoriously defending the cause of Christ and of Christians condemned unjustly, but still more broadly by also assuring all-powerful assistance to the Apostles in all their efforts and in their struggles against the world.[30]

The word "paraclesis" should not be translated as "consolation." Properly, it means "encouragement," "support," "assistance," and sometimes "exhortation." Paraclete is occasionally translated as the "Comforter" or the "Advocate." But the former of these two words is much too weak, and the latter restricts the role of the Spirit as Paraclete to an area or function that is too narrow. "Counsellor" would also be inadequate. It would be preferable to say "assessor" or "strengthener."

Our Lord was about to leave His disciples. Apparently they could no longer rely upon His help. And

[30] Luke 2:25; 1:6-24; Acts 4:36; 9:31; 13:15; 15:31; Rom. 12:8; 15:4-5; 1 Cor. 14:3; 2 Cor. 1:3, 5, 6, 7; 7:4; 8:4, 17; Philip. 2:1; 1 Thess. 2:3; 2 Thess. 2:16; 1 Tim. 4:13; Philemon 7; Heb. 6:18; 12:5; 13:32.

who would now guide them "in the way" that leads to "the place" which Jesus would prepare for them in the presence of the Father? It was "a new Paraclete, a new source of strength," the Holy Spirit Himself, who would continue the work begun by Jesus:

> If you love me, keep my commandments. And I will ask the Father and he will give you another Advocate to dwell with you forever, the Spirit of truth whom the world cannot receive (John 14:15-17).[31]

This Spirit is a "Spirit of Truth," who would reveal to them the glory of Jesus living with His Father (John 14:17-21). Furthermore, He would even ensure a mysterious return of Jesus in the midst of His disciples (John 14:21-24). Through His assistance the disciples would be able to perform still greater works, if possible, than those already performed by Jesus during His mortal life. Jesus Himself would come to perform them through His followers (John 14:11-14).

One of the prerogatives of the Paraclete would be to inspire witness to the Word:

> These things I have spoken to you while yet dwelling with you. But the Advocate, the Holy Spirit, whom the Father will send in my name, he will teach you all things, and bring to your mind whatever I have said to you (John 14:25-26).

[31] Our Lord Himself has been, up to now, the Paraclete, the support and guide of the Apostles. Henceforth, He will perform this function on the juridical level, one might say, before the Father, intervening like a *witness,* sure of being heard (1 John 2:1; Luke 12:8).

In the second part[32] of the discourse following the Last Supper, we find the same prophecy once more. The Spirit is again mentioned twice. The Spirit's support and help would be, in one sense, similar to juridical assistance, with the Spirit helping the disciples in their role as witnesses in the eternal trial of Jesus. But the Spirit would also sustain them in their struggles, "testifying" with them and giving them His strength:

> If the world hates you, know that it has hated me before you. . . . But because you are not of the world, but I have chosen you out of the world, therefore the world hates you. But when the Advocate has come, whom I will send you from the Father, the Spirit of truth who proceeds from the Father, he will bear witness, because from the beginning you are with me (John 15:18-19, 26-27).[33]

It was good for the disciples, therefore, that Jesus left them; thus the Spirit, an all-powerful witness and helper, was given to them:

> But I speak the truth to you; it is expedient for you that I depart. For if I do not go, the Advocate will not come to you; but if I go, I will send him to you. And when he has come he will convict the world of sin, and of justice, and of judgment: of sin, because they do not believe in me; of justice, because I go to the Father, and you will see me no more;

[32] Which is perhaps the first. As a matter of fact, John 15:1-16, 33 seems to certain authors to be a complement of the discourse after the Last Supper. In order to have a better sequence of thoughts and developments, it would be better to read 15:1-16, 33 between verses 13-31a and 31b, at the very beginning of the discourse.

[33] It will be noted that in the Synoptics (Mark 13:11; Matt. 10:19-20; Luke 12:11-12) the Paraclete-Spirit comes to bear witness in the trial of the world against the Christian. For John, on the other hand, He bears witness within the Christian, for the Christian is the judge in this new trial.

> and of judgment, because the prince of this world has already been judged (John 16:7-11).

Thus the three protagonists of Christ's trial—the world, Jesus Christ and the devil—are mentioned, and the role of the Paraclete is to keep the facts and data of this trial forever relevant. The world is condemned because it does not believe. Christ is justified because He has returned to the Father. And the devil is really the one condemned in this trial.

The disciples could not yet fully understand these things any more than all the rest that Jesus delayed telling them at that time, but the Spirit would guide them, opening the way that leads to all truth:

> Many things yet I have to say to you, but you cannot bear them now. But when he, the Spirit of truth, has come, he will teach you all the truth (John 16:12-13).

John, recording the sayings of Jesus which had been his meditation for many years, gave us this excellent definition of the role and function of the Holy Spirit. He is an all-powerful defender, a witness who will prolong the trial of the Messias, unjustly condemned, in order to prove the justice of His cause. This trial will take place deep in the conscience of every believer, and before the perpetually unjust tribunal of the world down through all the centuries. When believers themselves are attacked in their turn, the Holy Spirit will be there to sustain them. He will assist them in bearing witness for Jesus whenever they unite themselves to the sufferings of Christ, leading them to ultimate victory. The Spirit, who will reveal

Christ's victory and glory, and gradually all the wonders of the Christian mystery, will give them unshakable confidence, strength and peace during their pilgrimage to the Father (John 16:19-26; 17:1-26).

It seems that John, in the very discourse of the Lord, follows the earlier example of Paul and Peter, by appealing to the spiritual experience of those for whom his Gospel was intended.

Perhaps it was John who had something urgent to say, interrupting the sequence of the Lord's promises in order to intervene in his own name, when he wrote of the Spirit: "But you shall know him, because he will dwell with you, and be in you" (John 14:17).

The message of the discourse after the Last Supper, along with that of the Synoptics (Mark 13:11; Matt. 10:20; Luke 12:11-12) and the whole experience of the Apostles, rejoins the message of the Old Testament, which shows the Hebrews guided by the breath of the Spirit of God in the journey of return from exile (Is. 43:7). However, it is a path of truth that the Spirit must open up to Christians as He leads them to the Father.

It is, moreover, remarkable that the Holy Spirit, in perfect continuity with His role in the Old Testament as the spirit of God or as the wind driving the people toward fulfillment of their destiny, remains fundamentally and irretrievably opposed to the earthly world, and that His essential role as a "witness" and "paraclete" is to assist the Christian in his own opposition to the world, with the resulting consequences.

Accordingly, we see that the prophetic witnessing of the Apostles who proclaim the fulfillment of the prophecies, the moral witnessing of the martyrs who confess the name of the Lord, and the juridical witnessing provided by the Christian in the trial of the Lord, constitute a triple activity inspired by the Paraclete. The Christian must never lose sight of this triple resonance of his witness and its explicit reference to the Holy Spirit.

3. THE MINISTER

Besides the general function of witnessing, the Spirit of God animates the particular function of the ministry. Paul's experience is perhaps the most explicit example of this animation of the "ministers of Christ" by His Spirit. It will enable us to set forth the problem before making a closer study of the relationship between the ministry of the apostolate, or any other ministry, and the Holy Spirit.

a) *Paul, minister of the Spirit*

Around 52, during his second voyage, Paul wrote to the Christians of Thessalonica whom he had but recently left. He said:

> We know, brethren, beloved of God, how you were chosen. For our gospel was not delivered to you in word only, but in power also, and in the Holy Spirit, and in much fulness, as indeed you know what manner of men we have been among you for your sakes. And you became imitators of us and of the Lord, receiving the word in great tribulation, with joy of the Holy Spirit, so that you became a pattern to all the

believers in Macedonia and in Achaia (1 Thess. 1:4-7; cf. 2 Thess. 2:13-14).

Toward 55, during his third mission, St. Paul wrote to the Corinthians:

> And I was with you in weakness and in fear and in much trembling. And my speech and my preaching were not in the persuasive words of wisdom, but in the demonstration of the Spirit and of power, that your faith might rest, not on the wisdom of men, but on the power of God . . . (1 Cor. 2:3-5).
>
> Now we have received not the spirit of the world, but the spirit that is from God, that we may know the things that have been given us by God. These things we also speak, not in words taught by human wisdom, but in the learning of the Spirit, combining spiritual with spiritual (1 Cor. 2:12-13).[34]

Some time later he wrote them again:

> Clearly you are a letter of Christ, composed by us, written not with ink but with the Spirit of the living God, not on tablets of stone but on fleshly tablets of the heart (2 Cor. 3:3).

In view of all the marvels accomplished by the Spirit, Paul, from that time forth, considered his entire apostolic labor as the "ministry of the Spirit" (2 Cor. 3:8): a far more glorious ministry than the one which had been entrusted to Moses, one which constituted Paul's whole

[34] It is often very difficult to determine, in the apostolic letters as well as throughout the New Testament, when one is to read "spirit" and when "Spirit." In New Testament language, the word "pneuma" denotes the Spirit, the Third Person of the Trinity, sanctifying grace, or even a particular actual grace, when it is not referring to the breath of the wind, the soul, the spiritual part of our being, or a particular "disposition of spirit." The word is also used to designate the impure spirits or those spiritual creatures which are the angels. Compare with what we have said about "ruah," the Hebrew equivalent of "pneuma."

glory, powerful in the very measure of his own weakness, thanks to the Spirit.

When he wrote to the Romans in 57, at the end of his letter he summed up as follows all the apostolic labors to which he had up to then given himself:

> But I have written to you rather boldly here and there, brethren—as it were to refresh your memory—because of the grace that has been given me by God, that I should be a minister of Christ Jesus to the Gentiles; sanctifying the gospel of God, that the offering up of the Gentiles may become acceptable, being sanctified by the Holy Spirit. I have therefore this boast in Christ Jesus as regards the work of God. For I do not make bold to mention anything but what Christ has wrought through me to bring about the obedience of the Gentiles, by word and deed, with mighty signs and wonders, by the power of the Holy Spirit, so that from Jerusalem round about as far as Illyricum I have completed the evangelization of Christ (Rom. 15:15-19; cf. Heb. 2:4).

God's word, preached by the Apostle and heard by the faithful, seemed to him so linked up with the Spirit that he calls it, in his letter to the Ephesians, "the sword of the spirit" (Eph. 6:17), an essential part of the armor of the servant of God against the forces of evil.

It remains for us to consider more intimately the components of this ministry of the Spirit.

b) *the envoys and the Envoy*[35]

The basic group which ultimately structures the entire ministry of the Spirit is unquestionably that of the Apos-

35 There are some very profound views on the cooperation between the apostolic institution and the Holy Spirit in Congar, "Le Saint-Esprit et le

tles. They appear, particularly as a unit, as Christ's authorized representatives. Jewish law had established some very precise precedents on this point: when the "father of a family" was leaving his house for some time, a servant or a group of servants managed it in his place with full powers, just as if they were the real proprietors. This "proxy" or "sheliah" is clearly the type of servant Christ wished to set up as His replacement. As a matter of fact, it is noteworthy that the Apostles exercised powers only to the extent that Christ disappeared, and that the powers which they received from Christ are explicitly described as the powers of Christ:

> As the Father has sent me, so also I send you (John 20:21; cf. 17:18).
>
> He who receives you, receives me; and he who receives me, receives him who sent me (Matt. 10:40).

In effect, the powers of leading into the Kingdom and of remitting sins (Luke 24:45-49; John 20:22-23; Matt. 16:19) are transmitted to the "authorized representatives," according to the juridical rules, at the time of Christ's departure.

It is moreover significant that a certain number of parables which describe the role of servants in the Church establish the latter's activity to be during the absence of the father of the family and until his return.[36]

Corps Apostolique, réalisateurs de l'oeuvre du Christ," *R. Sc. Ph. Th.*, 1952, 613-625; 1953, 24-48.

[36] Matt. 25:14-25; 24:42-47; Mark 13:33-37. These three Gospels are still in use as the Gospel text in the Mass for Confessor Pontiffs, to celebrate the priesthood of the bishops, entrusted with power by Christ during His absence.

The Greek term ἀποστολος, "envoy," was adopted by very early Christian tradition to designate these "authorized representatives." It is in this managing of Christ's wealth in His stead that one finds the first foundation of the apostolic powers of the "envoys."[37]

However, in contrast to the simple Jewish proxy who substitutes for his master by a simple juridical agreement, the Christ-proxy, who is the envoy, finds the source of his power not only in a juridical mandate from his master who sends him forth, but within himself, in a new existence: that conferred on him by the Spirit. Finally, it is because he has the Spirit that the apostle can say that he is the authorized representative of Christ. The Spirit is the living link which unites Christ and His envoys; He is the final justification of the apostolic powers. Also, He accompanies every transfer of power:

> Receive the Holy Spirit; whose sins you shall forgive, they are forgiven them; and whose sins you shall retain, they are retained (John 20:22-23).

It is under the action of the Spirit that the Apostles are chosen (Acts 1:2; 13:2-4); in their decision and their preaching, they feel that they are perfectly one with the Spirit:

> We are witnesses of these things, and so is the Holy Spirit (Acts 5:32).
> The Holy Spirit and we have decided . . . (Acts 15:28).

37 Cf. the first chapter of Colson, *Les fonctions ecclésiales aux deux premiers siècles,* Desclée de Brouwer, 1957.

Actually, it is the Holy Spirit who is Christ's principal proxy, the Envoy par excellence. And it is precisely because the Spirit is the authorized representative par excellence that Christ must go away so that the former can exercise His role:

> It is expedient for you that I depart. For if I do not go, the Advocate will not come to you; but if I go, I will send him to you (John 16:7; cf. John 7:39).

> He will not speak on his own authority, but whatever he will hear he will speak. . . . He will glorify me, because he will receive of what is mine and declare it to you (John 16:13-14).

The hierarchy of the Church could have taken on a dynastic character which, beginning with "the brethren of Jesus," would have devolved, through the transmission of blood, on all the descendants of Christ. This was probably the momentary illusion of a part of the Jerusalem community concerning James, the cousin of Jesus, heir to the blood of David, the returned Messias. That is the way it had been at the death of Judas Machabeus (1 Mac. 3). But the hierarchy of the Church is not dynastic, and its unity is not achieved through the transmission of blood; it is spiritual and only the envoys of the Spirit participate in it. The ancient opposition between the flesh and the spirit finds here a fulfilment of considerable scope. It is also necessary to stress the reappearance in these "envoys" of the old theme which made the wind the "messenger" of God.

c) *After the Apostles*

It was not long before subordinate functions appeared around the representatives who shared the ministry of the Spirit. This is not the place to indicate their specific roles and characteristics.[38] Nevertheless, let us note—we shall return to this in a special paragraph[39]—that the new functions of Christianity: πρεσβύτεροι, ἐπίσκοποι, διδάσκαλες, etc., belong to the hierarchy of the synagogue and not to the hierarchy of the Temple. In other words, they derive from the "worship in spirit" as it was thought out and structured in Judaism in contrast to the exterior worship of the Temple. It is not to be wondered at that these ministers of spiritual worship become in the Church the ministers of the Spirit. It is indeed through the Spirit that Christians acceded to these responsibilities: Paul recalled this to the presbyters of Miletus:

> Take heed to yourselves and to the whole flock in which the Holy Spirit has placed you as bishops, to rule the Church of God, which he has purchased with his own blood (Acts 20:28).

A similar remark is addressed to Timothy:

> For this reason I admonish thee to stir up the grace of God which is in thee by the laying on of my hands. For God has not given us the spirit of fear, but of power and of love and of prudence (2 Tim. 1:6-7; cf. 1:14).

[38] Cf. Colson, *op. cit.*; Menoud, *L'Eglise et les ministères selon le Nouveau Testament,* Delachaux, 1949.

[39] Cf. *infra,* p. 144.

Generally, too, it is the Spirit who distributes ministries in the Church (1 Cor. 12:1, 31; Eph. 4:11-16):

> Now there are varieties of gifts, but the same Spirit; and there are varieties of ministries, but the same Lord; and there are varieties of workings, but the same God, who works all things in all.

We shall return later to this important text.

d) *Conclusion*

The Holy Spirit was not content simply to take the place of the prophetic spirit of the Old Testament. While respecting the laws of the inspiration of the men of God, He succeeded in raising the latter to the most spiritual functions of Christ's Lordship.

As Paraclete, He supports the witness of the Christians, giving them assurance of the fulfillment of the prophecies, inviting them to press this witness even to martyrdom, and, in any event, to the living confession of the Lord's name. But this witness itself rests on an event and must be transmitted. As envoy, therefore, the Holy Spirit animates a whole hierarchy of powers and, in cooperation with the latter, organizes the work of Christ from the time of His departure until He returns.

But these witnesses, these prophets, these envoys and representatives who collaborate with the Holy Spirit in the multiple ministries are, to be sure, only exercising the messianic prerogatives of the new King. Is it not time now to see at closer hand this new Prophet par excellence, the Messias?

4. THE MESSIAS

At the time of their first preaching, the Apostles restricted their scope to the most recent and most decisive events of the Lord's life, stressing the part played by the Spirit in the glorification of Christ and asking men to dispose themselves to receive the Spirit sent by the glorified Christ (Acts 2:14-41). Paul himself would be particularly sensitive to the experience of the Holy Spirit through his ministry. Soon, however, the framework of apostolic preaching expanded and the Apostles were pleased to relate all the actions of power and of goodness performed by Jesus during His mortal life under the influence of the Spirit whose "Anointed One" He was, even before His glorification (Acts 10:37-38; cf. Acts 2:21-22).

Thus it came to be that the experience which the Christian community had of the Holy Spirit was synthesized around the person of Christ as around the true source of these charisms, and the Apostles' theological reflections gradually tended to make of the Spirit which animated them, the Spirit of Christ Himself.

Where the initial preaching associated the gift of the Spirit with Christ and His resurrection, the later preaching, as reported in the synoptic tradition, was already content to trace the first-fruits of this gift back to the baptism of Christ, and Luke echoes another tradition according to which this gift goes back even to the events of the Incarnation. We shall quickly review these traditions in order to discover therein what might serve our purposes here.

Let us recall first of all that in the eyes of Isaias, the Messias is clothed with the Spirit of God (Is. 11:1-2; cf. 42:1; 61:1) because He is, in the prophet's view, the personalized synthesis of the different charisms of the spirit distributed all through the ancient dispensation, and His mission is to establish the kingdom wherein these charisms will finally be accomplished and fulfill their purpose.[40] In the traditions we are going to analyze, then, we can expect to discover—to the extent that these traditions wish to remain faithful to the ancient messianic theology—a concern for seeing accomplished in the person of Christ His messianic investiture by the Spirit, and the royal diffusion of the gifts of this Spirit.

a) *The Investiture of the Messias at the Resurrection*[41]

The resurrection of Christ consists essentially in the insufflation of a new "breath of life" into His mortal flesh:

> Put to death indeed in the flesh, he was brought to life in the spirit (1 Pet. 3:18).

Two interpretations immediately arose in the apostolic tradition regarding this essential fact of the re-spiritualization of Christ. Christ thereby receives a breath of life which He transmits to all the living, as Adam had

[40] Cf. *supra*, p. 41.

[41] Cf. Schmitt, *Jésus ressuscité dans la prédication apostolique*, Gabalda, 1949, pp. 175-214.

once received in vain a breath of life to be transmitted: this is the theme of Christ the new Adam (1 Cor. 15:42-49), which we shall study further on. But Christ, in thus receiving the Spirit, in some way undergoes His own investiture as Messias:

> . . . concerning his Son who was born to him according to the flesh of the offspring of David; who was foreordained Son of God by an act of power in keeping with the holiness of his spirit, by resurrection from the dead, Jesus Christ our Lord (Rom. 1:1-4).[42]

And it was precisely with the Resurrection as the messianic investiture that Peter's first preaching dealt:

> This Jesus God has raised up, and we are all witnesses of it. Therefore, exalted by the right hand of God, and receiving from the Father the promise of the Holy Spirit, he has poured forth this Spirit . . . (Acts 2:32-33).

And, to show clearly that this was indeed a messianic investiture, Peter framed this statement with the description of the Messias' ascent to His royal throne, a throne now removed to heaven at the right hand of the Father (Acts 2:19-36). In receiving the anointing of the Spirit in His resurrection, Christ received the right of ascending the throne of David, raised up unto the Father, fulfilling the messianic promise, "Your own offspring I will set upon your throne" (cf. Ps. 131:11).

Thus, the resurrection and ascension of Christ are the two stages of His messianic investiture, and Pentecost is the first manifestation of the exercise by the Lord of His

[42] Royal title of the Messias and of the Kings of Israel.

royal prerogatives in the diffusion of the Spirit of the last times.

b) *The investiture of the Messias at His baptism*

Let us recall the final moments the Apostles spent with Jesus. They had gathered in the Cenacle. At the moment He takes His leave from them, Jesus draws their attention to an event of His earthly life which was the first of those to which they had been witnesses:

> And while eating with them, he charged them not to depart from Jerusalem, but to wait for the promise of the Father, "of which you have heard," said he, "by my mouth; for John indeed baptized with water, but you shall be baptized with the Holy Spirit not many days hence" (Acts 1:4-5; cf. Luke 24:29; John 1:33).

This "promise of the Father" is unquestionably linked not only to all the announcements of the Old Testament pertaining to the outpouring of the Spirit, but also to the spiritual event in the life of Jesus which holds the most important place in the synoptic tradition: the baptism of Jesus by John after the preaching of the Baptist in the desert, and the descent of the Spirit on Jesus.

If we examine all the traditions which underlie the three synoptic Gospels, it indeed seems as though the public life of Jesus is presented therein, at least tacitly, as if it unfolded between two outstanding manifestations of the Spirit. At the beginning of the Lord's ministry, the Spirit descends on Jesus at the time of His baptism; the baptism of the Spirit thus followed the baptism of water, for Christ. At the end of His public life, Jesus, according to the testimony of the Gospel of Matthew, sent His disciples into the whole world to baptize "in the name of the Father, and of the Son, and of the Holy Spirit" (Matt. 28:19). Likewise, Luke ends his Gospel with the final words of Christ announcing the sending, in the near future, of "the promise of my Father" (Luke 24:49).[43]

[43] The question of Mark must be considered separately, since the finale is missing in a large number of manuscripts, and the canonical, inspired finale seems as though it could be considered a resumé of the Gospel according to Luke. One of the non-canonical endings of the Gospel according to Mark also concludes with an almost explicit reference to the gift of the Spirit: "I was handed over to death for those who have sinned, so that they might be converted to the Truth, so that they might inherit the spiritual and incorruptible glory of that Justice which is in heaven."

This arrangement of the synoptic Gospels is significant. In the eyes of the Apostles, their Lord was anointed with the messianic Spirit at the Resurrection, and, since Pentecost, has been giving this Spirit to His followers through Baptism. This, now, is where the synoptic catechesis partially relates the messianic investiture of Christ to His baptism. It was all the more drawn to doing so by the fact that the experience of Christian Baptism in the Spirit was a sure guide. But it is important to note that, even while thus anticipating the messianic investiture of Christ, this tradition does so only with explicit reference to the Paschal and Pentecostal mystery of the Lord. This is why the Gospels which begin with the account of the messianic investiture at Baptism do not hesitate to terminate with the announcement of this full investiture on

Pentecost Sunday. This is why, too, in the very account of the baptism of Christ, there is a reminder of the future baptism in the Spirit and in fire as being far more perfect:

> I indeed baptize you with water. But one mightier than I is coming . . . He will baptize you with the Holy Spirit and with fire (Luke 3:16; cf. Matt. 3:11).

This is a prophecy which Luke hastens to recall at the time of its fulfillment:

> For John indeed baptized with water, but you shall be baptized with the Holy Spirit not many days hence (Acts 1:5).

Thus, there is a two-fold interpretation of Christ's baptism in the Jordan. On the one hand, one must see in it the fulfilment of the events and of the messianic signs of the Old Testament, without, however, losing sight of the relationship between the baptism of Christ and His true coronation in His death and resurrection. The messianic investiture in the Jordan is an inauguration whose consummation remains linked to the mystery of Easter and of Pentecost. It is precisely from this perspective that one must read the account of the investiture in the Jordan:[44]

> . . . When all the people had been baptized, Jesus also having been baptized and being in prayer . . . heaven was opened, and the Holy Spirit descended upon him in bodily form as a dove, and a voice came from heaven, "Thou art my beloved Son, in thee I am well pleased" (Luke 3:21-22).

[44] A principle well-established by Riesenfeld, "La signification sacramentaire du baptême johannique," *Dieu vivant,* no. 13, 29-38.

Why did the Spirit appear in a bodily shape like that of a dove at the time of Jesus' baptism? A text of Peter's first epistle (1 Pet. 3:20; 4:6) may help us to determine this. Baptism is compared therein to a new deluge which submerges a condemned world, so that a restored mankind may be born. It falls to the dove, in the Genesis account, to signify that the new world has been born (Gen. 8:10-11). The dove which hovers over Christ also recalls the flight of the "ruâh," the wind of the divine "Spirit," above the waters in the account of the Creation (Gen. 1:2), though the Babylonian origins of the account would incline one rather to think that the primitive sense of the text was a more material order.

The most important element of this ceremony, however, the one which most clearly gives it its messianic character, is the "voice from heaven." This voice was a vital element in the ancient ceremony of royal investiture,[45] an echo of which has been preserved for us in Psalm 2:

> I will proclaim the decree of the Lord: the Lord said to me, "You are my son; this day I have begotten you" (Ps. 2:7; cf. Ps. 109:1).

This voice from heaven first of all applies to Christ the prophecy of the "servant" in Isaias (42:1). But, by playing on the double significance of the word παις, it substitutes the more royal and more messianic title of "son" for the word "servant." Also, Peter is able to compare this voice to the very anointing of investiture itself:

[45] Cf. Riesenfeld, *Le Christ transfiguré,* pp. 250-252.

> You know what took place throughout Judea; for he began in Galilee after the baptism preached by John; how God anointed Jesus of Nazareth with the Holy Spirit and with power . . . (Acts 10:37-38).

Immediately after the descent of the Spirit upon Him, Jesus, "driven by the Spirit," went into the desert to struggle victoriously there against evil and against its chieftain (Mark 1:12-13). Thus, under the impulse of the Spirit, which is nothing more here than the cloud and column of fire spiritualized,[46] Christ relives the experience of the desert which established the new people, even to the three fundamental temptations. But in the synoptic account, this theme of the desert is coupled with the messianic theme. The first and second temptations (Matt. 4:3-5) revolve around the title "Son of God," and the third (Matt. 4:9) centers around a temporal messianity. It was enough for the Lord to reveal that His messianic nature is born in humility and obedience, for Him to win His first messianic victory over Satan, in close combat, through the power of the Spirit. Throughout the synoptic Gospels, these repeated victories over Satan constitute the irrefutable proof that He is indeed the Messias, the anointed one charged with establishing the kingdom of God.

When John, for his part, takes up the account of the baptism of Christ, he introduces certain nuances. Not only does the fourth Gospel say that the Spirit descended upon Jesus at the time of His baptism, but, on two oc-

[46] Cf. *supra*, p. 45.

casions, that "it abode upon him" (John 1:32-24). By adding this feature which has the value of a sign, John is insisting on the fulness of the Spirit dwelling in Jesus. He is therefore the "Chosen One" of whom the prophecies of the book of Isaias speak (cf. John 3:34):

And the spirit of the Lord shall rest upon him (Is. 11:2; cf. 42:1; 61:1).

c) *The exercise of Christ's spiritual messianity*

Having received the Spirit at His resurrection, and having been consecrated Messias by this anointing, Christ immediately exercised His new royalty in the outpouring of Pentecost. Such was the outline of primitive preaching. Since the Spirit anointed the Messias even before His public life, the exercise of His messianity must have its effect throughout all this public life. Thus, it can be said that in the eyes of the Synoptics, the public life of Christ was but the putting into practice of His investiture by the Spirit, in the same way that Pentecost is but the putting into practice of Easter.

Each one of the Synoptics, in his own way, invoked this spiritual messianity of Christ.

For Mark, it appears above all in the victories of the Christ-Messias over the unclean spirits.[47] There is, as a matter of fact, absolute opposition between the two spirits (Mark 3:22-30). Jesus soon associates all His followers with this struggle (Mark 6:7), but the Apostles do not immediately know how to be victorious (Mark 9:14-29).

[47] Mark 1:23, 26, 27; 3:11, 30; 5:2, 8, 13; 6:7; 7:25; 11:17; 9:20, 25.

Indeed, the forces of evil can only be routed by prayer. True prayer, as we will soon learn, is the work of the Spirit. It is prayer, too, which obtains from the Father the coming of the Spirit.

Struggles are, moreover, foreseen for the future, before the final coming of the Son of Man; but the disciples of Jesus will enjoy in that event a very special assistance on the part of the Holy Spirit (Mark 13:11).

Thus, the Gospel according to Mark appears as the account of the victorious battles waged by Jesus, "driven" and animated by the Spirit. In Mark's finale, where the other Synoptics announce the sending of the Spirit, he is content to announce to the Apostles that they will triumph over the wicked spirits:

> In my name they shall cast out devils; they shall speak in new tongues; they shall take up serpents; and if they drink any deadly thing, it shall not hurt them; they shall lay hands upon the sick and they shall get well (Mark 16:17-18).

Mark characteristically stresses that the only powers which the Apostles will have so long as the Lord is alive are solely powers of this type—directly oriented to the struggle against the evil spirits (Mark 6:7; 9:14-29)—and the outline Christ gives them of their post-Pentecost powers is centered exclusively along this line, as if all the apostolic powers were summed up in triumphing over the forces of evil. This, unquestionably, is the ancient opposition between the wind and the earth, the breath and the flesh, manifested now between the Spirit and the spirits of the world. But this opposition has now become the very substance of the messianic struggle. The *Manual of Discipline* recently discovered at the monastery of Qumrân, contains a document which describes precisely the eschatological war between the Spirit of God and the evil spirits.[48] In the light of these texts, it seems that one of the concerns of Christ is that of forming an army of the Spirit of God through the intermediary of the powers He turns over to His Apostles, for it was announced that it will not be until the end of time that the army of the Spirit of God will overcome the army of the evil spirits. Thus, the Apostles are the direct descendants of those soldiers strengthened by the Spirit of God to conquer Satan through the possession of the Promised Land: Samson, Gideon, etc.

Matthew is no less sensitive than Mark to the episodes in the struggle between the two spirits. He repeats practically all of Mark's texts on this subject, with this single original feature, that he places this ministry of Christ under the action of one of the prophecies of the Servant who is "meek and humble of heart":

> "Behold, my servant, whom I have chosen, my beloved in whom my soul is well pleased: I will put my Spirit upon him and he will declare judgment to the Gentiles. He will not wrangle, nor cry aloud . . . A bruised reed he will not break, and a smoking wick he will not quench, till he send forth judgment unto victory; and in his name will the Gentiles hope" (Matt. 12:18-21; cf. Is. 42:1-4).

48 Lambert's translation, in *NRT*, 1951, 958-976; commentary by Dupont-Sommer, "L'instruction sur les deux esprits dans le manuel de discipline," *R.H.R.*, 1952, 5-35; Daniélou, "La doctrine des deux esprits," *Dieu vivant*, no. 25, 1953, 127-236.

Luke also recalls, at the very outset of the public ministry of Jesus, the prophecies which announce the very special bond which unites God's Anointed, the Messias, with the Spirit of the Lord. He, too, cites the prophecies of the "Servant," but selects passages which specifically announce His spiritual power manifesting the miracles of Jesus:

> The Spirit of the Lord is upon me because he has anointed me; to bring good news to the poor he has sent me, to proclaim to the captives release, and sight to the blind; to set at liberty the oppressed, to proclaim the acceptable year of the Lord (Luke 4:18; cf. Is. 61:1-2).[49]

Luke is less insistent than Mark and Matthew on the power of Jesus as manifested by His control over the unclean spirits. He does not stress in the same way the value, as an irrefutable sign of the messianic dignity of Jesus, deriving from the victory He wins over them. In this respect, it suffices to compare Luke 12:8-10 with Matthew 12:31-32 and Mark 3:28-29.

It is above all the miracles of goodness wrought by Jesus that won over this physician (Luke 4:23; 5:12-26; 6:18).

More than all the others, however, he insists on the sway held by the Spirit of God over Jesus. When Jesus returns from the desert, Luke tells us:

[49] Matthew puts his Gospel under the impulse of Isaias 42:1-4 and Luke under that of Isaias 61:1-2; it will be noted that both merely repeat the literary sources of the account of the baptism, clear proof of their desire to extend their commentary on it throughout the life of Christ.

> And Jesus returned in the power of the spirit into Galilee; and the fame of him went out through the whole country. And he taught in their synagogues, and was honored by all (Luke 4:14-15).

Luke was to use similar terms in describing the activity of the Apostles moved by the Spirit after Pentecost, and the favor in which they were held by the people (cf. Acts 2:46-47; 5:31-35).

Thus, the Easter-in-anticipation constituted by the baptism of Christ in the Jordan was followed, during the entire course of the Messias' life, by a Pentecost manifested especially in the powers exercised by Jesus and transmitted by Him with respect to the evil spirits. For a long time, it was these powers over devils in the healing of the sick and the forgiveness of sins which, in the eyes of the primitive community, provided the clearest proof that the messianic kingdom had arrived.

d) *Messianic investiture from the time of the Incarnation*

It is Luke's merit that he preserved a tradition of the Judeo-Christian community according to which the Pentecost just experienced by the primitive Church was already the lot of this community even during the events surrounding and preparing for the birth of the Messias (Luke 1, 2). Matthew had already solemnly associated the Holy Spirit with this mystery of the Incarnation:

> When Mary his mother had been betrothed to Joseph, before they came together, she was found to be with child by

> the Holy Spirit. . . . An angel of the Lord appeared to him in a dream saying: "Do not be afraid, Joseph, son of David, to take to thee Mary thy wife, for that which is begotten in her is of the Holy Spirit" (Matt. 1:18-20).

Luke relates the same facts to us with greater detail, and already presents them, to some degree, in a Pentecostal atmosphere.

The whole environment in which Jesus appeared is shown to be animated by the Spirit, whether it is the Baptist and his mother who are involved, or even Zachary and, a fortiori, Mary; or, after the birth of Jesus, Simeon and Anna.

At the time of the announcement to Zachary, the divine messenger declares:

> Thy wife Elizabeth shall bear thee a son and thou shalt call his name John. And thou shalt have joy and gladness, and many will rejoice at his birth. For he shall be great before the Lord; he shall drink no wine or strong drink, and shall be filled with the Holy Spirit even from his mother's womb (Luke 1:13-15).

As for Jesus, His very conception is due to the action of the Holy Spirit. To Mary who asks:

"How shall this happen, since I do not know man?" (Luke 1:34), the angel replies:

> The Holy Spirit shall come upon thee, and the power of the Most High shall overshadow thee (Luke 1:35).

Mary and the child she bears possess the Holy Spirit in such fulness that at their very approach, and at the very sound of Mary's voice, the child in Elizabeth's womb leaps and Elizabeth is filled with the Holy Spirit:

> When Elizabeth heard the greeting of Mary . . . the babe in her womb leapt. And Elizabeth was filled with the Holy Spirit . . . (Luke 1:41).

After the birth of the Baptist, Zachary himself, seized in turn by the Spirit, prophesies:

> Zachary his father was filled with the Holy Spirit, and prophesied . . . (Luke 1:67).

Nevertheless, it is not explicitly stated in this account that the "Spirit rests" upon Jesus, prior to the day of His investiture on the banks of the Jordan at the time of His baptism, but only "the grace of God"; nor is it explicitly said that the "Spirit" filled Him, but rather "Wisdom." This episode of the baptism, as a matter of fact, occupies a position of foremost importance in the primitive outlines of Christian history. Both Luke and Matthew wish to place this spiritual investiture of the Messias in full relief. It is enough for them to have traced the beginnings of Pentecost, as it were, back to the point where the two Testaments meet.

Indeed, if the Holy Spirit fills John the Baptist, it is to make of him a prophet similar to Samuel, once charged with designating and anointing David as King-Messias. For is not the Baptist charged with designating Him who is to sit on the throne of David? (Compare Luke 1:15 and 1 Kings 1 and 16.)[50]

50 Cf. Th. Maertens, *Le Messie est là*, pp. 21 ff.

The Holy Spirit descends upon the Virgin as He descended upon Othoniel (Jdg. 3:10), on Jephte (Jdg. 11:29), on David (1 Kings 19:23), in order to give her the strength to conceive within her womb a savior, the offspring of David, of whom the prophets said that the Spirit would rest on Him. He "overshadows" her, as a cloud, impelled by the force of the wind, covered with "its shadow" the tent of God during the Exodus (Ex. 24:15-18; cf. 1 Rom. 8:10-13).

The spirit which animates the parentage and the entourage of the child Jesus is a spirit of prophecy, the source of the inspiration which put "the word" into the mouth of the ancient prophets. When Elizabeth is touched by the Spirit, she prophesies; soon Zachary will prophesy in turn (Luke 1:67), and so will Simeon who comes to the Temple "driven by the Spirit," as by the wind. All three, like the Virgin, speak rhythmically, in words similar to the oracles and inspired canticles of the ancient prophets (Luke 1:46-55; 1:29-32).

In the text of the Gospel according to Luke, possession by the Spirit appears to be contagious, as it had been of old, in the days of the "nabis" and of the prophet Samuel (1 Kings 10:5; 19:23) and even in the days of Moses (Num. 11:24-29), and also as it was in the Church of the early Christian era (Acts 5:31; 11:14).

In the early chapters of Luke, everything takes place in an atmosphere which recalls both that of the old texts which describe for us the gestures and actions of the "prophets of old," and the spiritual atmosphere in which, according to the Book of Acts, the new prophets, the members of the Church of the very earliest Christian period, lived and acted.

At the center of this spiritual outpouring attested to by the accounts collected by Luke, is the Virgin, just as he presented her to us in the midst of the Apostles, gathered in the upper chamber awaiting the coming of the Spirit (Acts 1:14). In her, the Spirit will give life to the first-born of all the members of the new world, just as later on, the extension of the person of Jesus, the mysterious body of Christ which is the Church, will be born in her presence and, as it were, in her.

The baptism of the Spirit begins with her, and the first Christian generations never stopped contemplating this mystery, in meditating on the prophecies of the Book of Isaias relative to Emmanuel and His mother (Is. 7:14; 11:1-3; 11:9).

e) *The messianic investiture in John*

This would seem to be the place to bring out a small detail which enables us to obtain from John a perspective which is slightly different from that of the Synoptics.

Where the first three Evangelists tell us, at the climax of Christ's Passion, that Jesus "breathed His last," "expired" (Luke 23:46; Mark 15:37) or "gave up his spirit" (Matt. 27:50), St. John uses a word which could mean that Jesus "transmitted" His spirit.

Thus he connects the moment when Jesus transmits to His followers the Spirit promised by the Father, with the moment of the Passion of Christ—the "hour of the Lord."

In John's view, therefore, Jesus has given the "living water" of the Spirit along with His blood, and in the same gesture (John 19:33-35). Of course, John does not ignore the fact of Pentecost, or that continuous Pentecost which is the life of the Church down through the ages, or the fact that the Spirit is to be given in a special manner to the Twelve (John 20:22-23). After His resurrection, Jesus appears to His assembled followers and sends them into the whole world, while giving them, with His own breath, the spirit of forgiveness and of condemnation of the world (John 20:21-23). But, as an eyewitness of the passion of Christ (John 19:35), John felt obliged to stress the profound value of the redemptive act and the primary origin of Christ's messianity.

5. CONCLUSION: THE SPIRIT OF THE KINGDOM

Throughout this chapter, we have assisted at the birth of various functions, all of them animated by the Holy Spirit: prophets, apostles, witnesses, all gather around the Messias in order to exploit with Him and through Him, the messianic gifts of the Spirit of God. Thus is verified the ancient prophecy:

> My spirit that is in thee and my words that I have put in thy mouth shall not depart out of thy mouth, nor out of the mouth of thy seed's seed, saith the Lord (Is. 59:21).

In this way, the final kingdom is organized, a kingdom characterized by the fulness of the Spirit given to all, in view of the new people God is causing to be reborn from its ashes under the action of His Spirit (Ezech. 37:1-14). The connection between the Kingdom and the Spirit is affirmed by the Synoptics:

> If I cast out devils by the Spirit of God, then the kingdom of God has come upon you (Matt. 12:28).

One can even discern in Luke the intent to substitute the expression "Spirit" for the expression "Kingdom," which is, no doubt, in his view, too temporal:[51]

> "Lord, wilt thou at this time restore the kingdom to Israel?" But he said to them, "It is not for you to know the times or dates which the Father has fixed by his own authority; but you shall receive power when the Holy Spirit comes upon you . . . (Acts 1:6-7).

Just as He constituted the people around Moses in the desert, around David in the Promised Land, around the Messias in the prophetic visions, so the Spirit of God finally brings about this royalty by organizing and animating the different functions and structures of the Church. We shall have a great deal to say on this subject, but we must still assemble some other documents before permitting ourselves to synthesize the action of the Spirit on the Church.

51 Cf. Samain, "L'Esprit et le Royaume de Dieu," *Rev. dioc. Tourn.*, 1947, 481-492.

C

the New Covenant

The breath of God had brought, in the desert, the Law and the Covenant with God. This intervention was too external and too material to be truly effective; also, Ezechiel describes another intervention of the "breath of God," this one less external: a new "spirit" will be placed in man so that he may be able to observe the Law and conform to it.[52] This fundamental bond between the spirit of God and the Covenant was to be verified in the new dispensation; thus, it is possible to be assured in advance that the new Covenant concluded between God and His Church will be the doing of the Holy Spirit, and that He will observe in the establishing of this Covenant the laws which the spirit of God observed in setting up the old Covenant.

[52] Cf. *supra,* p. 55.

1. THE FEAST OF THE COVENANT

The Jews used to celebrate the Pasch for fifty days, and the fiftieth such day, "Pentecost," was a special commemoration of the transmission of the Law and of the inauguration of the Covenant.

"When the days of Pentecost were drawing to a close," (Acts 2:1), the Apostles, like all the Jews, remembered the sojourn of their fathers in the desert and the contact which they established then with the spirit of God, that spirit whose intervention in the first liberation and the first Covenant was underscored with growing insistence by the other inspired ones.

To celebrate a feast day, for the Jews as for us, was not merely to celebrate the remembrance of a past event, but to relive it in some way for oneself, to make its graces one's own.

In the Passover *Haggadah*, used by pious Jews during the paschal celebration, we read: "Each of us, down through the ages, has the duty of considering himself as if he had himself come forth from Egypt. For it is written [Ex. 13:8]: 'On this day you shall explain to your son, This is because of what the Lord did for me when *I came out* of Egypt.' It is not just our ancestors whom the Holy One—blessed be his name—has delivered; but He has also delivered us along with them. For it is written [Deut. 6:23] 'He brought *us* from there to lead *us* into the land he promised on oath to *our* fathers, and to give it to *us*.' This is why we have the duty of thanking, of singing, of praising, of glorifying, of exalting, of celebrating of blessing, of magnifying, and of honoring the one who has performed all these miracles for our ancestors and for us. He has led us from slavery toward freedom, from distress toward joy, from mourning toward the feast, from darkness toward the light, from servitude toward emancipation. In His honor, let us sing a new canticle, Alleluia." What the Jews say and think of Passover also holds true for the meaning they give to the liturgy of Pentecost and all the other festivals.

And that is not all: the feasts are not merely turned toward the past, but also toward the future. From century to century, the prophets announce a renewal, on a more profound and more beautiful level, of all the events of the past. As regards Pentecost, they announced to a new people of God after the exile the gift of a new Law under a new Covenant.

Thus, they imperceptibly substituted Sion for Sinai as the mount of the Covenant. Henceforth, it would be on Sion that the new Law would be given, that the new Covenant would be concluded and practiced by a people of saints. This substitution (which will become opposition in Paul's eyes: Gal. 4:21-31) began with the discovery of the "new law" or "Deuteronomy" on Sion (4 Kings 22-23), but was especially brought out through the perspective of the prophets (Is. 2:3). Moses and Aaron (Ps. 98:6) are included for the benefit of Sion, a new decalogue is composed for Sion (Ps. 14:1-4), and it is there that the community of the just is expected (Is. 9:21).

It is not surprising, therefore, when Christ enjoins His Apostles to remain in Jerusalem in order to seal the new Covenant which is definitively substituted for that of Sinai (Acts 1:4). Indeed, the wind from Sinai suddenly bursts upon Sion:

> And suddenly there came a sound from heaven, as of a violent wind blowing, and it filled the whole house (Acts 2:1; cf. Ex. 19:16-20).

In turn, fire, which was part of Sinai's theophany (Ex. 19:16-18), is revealed in the miracle of Pentecost:

> And there appeared to them parted tongues as of fire (Acts 2:3).

The feast of the Holy Spirit is also truly the feast of the New Law, the New Covenant.[53] We must now delve further into this relationship.

2. THE PAULINE EXPERIENCE

We have a unique guide in probing these relationships between the Spirit and the Law, in the person and experience of Paul. Let us follow his own testimony, all through his letters, before considering its main outlines.

a) *To the Thessalonians: The Spirit who sanctifies*

At the end of his second voyage, Paul wrote two letters to the Thessalonians. To encourage them, he

53 There are some fine spiritual considerations in Lecuyer, "Pentecôte et Loi nouvelle," *Vie. Spir.* 88, 1954, 471-490.

reminded them of the marvelous things the Holy Spirit had just accomplished in them:

> And you became imitators of us and of the Lord, receiving the word in great tribulation, with joy of the Holy Spirit, so that you became a pattern to all the believers in Macedonia and Achaia (1 Thess. 1:6).

Then he presented the gift of the Spirit to them as a requirement for sanctity and perfect purity, recommending that they make even greater progress:

> For this is the will of God, your sanctification . . . God has not called us unto uncleanness, but unto holiness. . . . Therefore, he who rejects these things rejects not man but God, who has also given his Holy Spirit to us (1 Thess. 4:3-8).

This last text is a quotation from Ezechiel 37:14, where the prophet announces that the spirit of God will lead the people in a new exodus toward the Promised Land. Thessalonica, too, is the beneficiary of this gift of the spirit to the Messias' people.

In the Second Epistle to the Thessalonians, Paul is mindful once again of all the fruits of grace and sanctification and salvation produced in them by the Spirit who is preparing them to share in the glory of Jesus. The gift of the Spirit seems to him to be wholly oriented toward the ultimate glory:

> But we, brethren beloved of God, are bound to give thanks to God always for you, because God has chosen you as the first-fruits unto salvation through the sanctification of the Spirit and belief of the truth. For this purpose he also called you by our preaching to gain the glory of our Lord Jesus Christ (2 Thess. 2:13-14).

b) *To the Corinthians: the spiritual law*

In the First Epistle to the Corinthians, Paul returns to the theme of sanctification through the Spirit, opposing it to the sins of the world in the name of the basic opposition between the Spirit and the world:

> Do not err: neither fornicators, nor idolaters, nor adulterers, nor the effeminate, nor sodomites, nor thieves, nor the covetous, nor drunkards, nor the evil-tongued, nor the greedy will possess the kingdom of God. And such were some of you, but you have been washed, you have been sanctified, you have been justified in the name of our Lord Jesus Christ, and in the Spirit of our God (1 Cor. 6:9-11).

But it is in the second letter that this sanctification is opposed for the first time to the sanctification which the law of Moses was able to effect.

Here now, at the outset, relying on the theme of the "spiritual law" in Ezechiel (24:12; 11:19; 36:26), the problem is posed:

> You are our letter [of commendation] written on our hearts, which is known and read by all men; clearly you are a letter of Christ, composed by us, written not with ink but with the Spirit of the living God, not on tablets of stone but on fleshly tablets of the heart (2 Cor. 3:2-3).

We are dealing here with a description of the apostolic ministry and of its fruit in the Spirit. Paul likes this type of description, but in this case he borrows a biblical image, the law written in the heart, and this image will lead him into a long digression on the opposition between the law of Moses and the spiritual law of the Spirit.

> He also it is who has made us fit ministers of the new covenant, not of the letter but of the spirit; for the letter kills, but the spirit gives life. Now if the ministration of death, which was engraved in letters upon stones, was inaugurated in such glory that the children of Israel could not look steadfastly upon the face of Moses on account of the transient glory that shone upon it, shall not the ministration of the spirit be still more glorious? (2 Cor. 3:5-8; cf. 17-18).

One senses that the theology of the spiritual law is quietly taking shape: it will be completed in the following Epistle.

c) *To the Galatians: freedom of the spirit and its fruits*

In the Second Epistle to the Corinthians, Paul had already indicated the bond which links possession of the Spirit of the Lord with freedom (2 Cor. 3:17). He returns to this theme more insistently in the Epistle to the Galatians. Paul is opposed to the Judaizers who would like to subject the disciples of Christ to the yoke of the Law. Fearing that the Galatians may be tempted by this doctrine, he calls upon their experience and asks them what has transformed them: the works of the Law, or the receiving of the Spirit granted to those who address themselves to the Lord with faith in the crucified Christ?

> O foolish Galatians, who has bewitched you, before whose eyes Jesus Christ has been depicted crucified? This only I would learn from you: Did you receive the Spirit in virtue of the works of the Law, or in virtue of hearing and believing? . . . Have you suffered so much in vain? He therefore who gives the Spirit to you, and works miracles among you, does he do it by the works of the Law, or by the message of faith? Even thus "Abraham believed God, and it was credited to him as justice" (Gal. 3:1-6).

> Christ redeemed us from the curse of the Law, becoming a curse for us . . . that the blessing of Abraham might come to the Gentiles through Christ Jesus, that through faith we might receive the promise of the Spirit (Gal. 3:13-14).

The opposition between the regime of the Law and that of the Spirit, which Paul had already set forth to the Corinthians, is taken up once again on a more profound level. The Law was given us in order to lead us to Christ, so that we might then be justified by faith, and when faith had come, we became sons of God: the Spirit, who makes us call God "Father" gives testimony to this:

> We too, when we were children, were enslaved under the elements of the world. But when the fullness of time came, God sent His Son, born of a woman, born under the Law, that he might redeem those who were under the Law, that we might receive the adoption of sons. And because you are sons, God has sent the Spirit of his Son into our hearts, crying, "Abba, Father." So that he is no longer a slave, but a son; and if a son, an heir also through God (Gal. 4:3-7).

It is at this point that the passage comes in which Paul contrasts Sinai and Sion, in a context we have already analyzed with regard to Pentecost as the feast of the Covenant (Gal. 4:21-31).

Later in the Epistle, Paul describes the entire Christian life as a journey under the guidance of the Spirit. To be sure, we still feel within us the burden of fleshly lusts, which the Law vainly tried of old to restrain, but the Spirit is there to help us make progress and to make us, freed now from the yoke of the Law and the flesh, produce fruit which is completely the opposite of th works of the flesh:

> For we in the Spirit wait for the hope of justice in virtue o faith. . . . you have been called to liberty, brethren; onl do not use liberty as an occasion for sensuality. . . . But I say Walk in the Spirit, and you will not fulfill the lusts of th flesh. For the flesh lusts against the spirit, and the spiri against the flesh; for these are opposed to each other, so tha you do not do what you would. But if you are led by th Spirit, you are not under the Law. Now the works of th flesh are manifest, which are immorality, uncleanness, licen tiousness . . . contentions . . . envies . . . And concerning thes I warn you, as I have warned you, that they who do suc things will not attain the kingdom of God. But the fruit of th Spirit is: charity, joy, peace, patience, kindness, goodness faith, modesty, continency. Against such things there is n law. And they who belong to Christ have crucified their flesh with its passions and desires. If we live by the Spirit, by the Spirit let us also walk. Let us not become desirous of vain-glory, provoking one another, envying one another (Gal. 5:5-26).

Paul, here, has presented the Spirit as the source of our life. He asks us to surrender to His animation and to His guidance. He attaches several warnings to his invitation:

> Be not deceived, God is not mocked. For what a man sows, that he will also reap. For he who sows in the flesh, from the flesh also will reap corruption. But he who sows in the spirit, from the spirit will reap life everlasting . . . (only) a new creation is of any account. And whoever follow this rule, peace and mercy upon them, even upon the Israel of God (Gal. 6:7-8; 15-16).

d) *To the Romans: the Spirit struggles against the flesh*

The Epistle to the Romans seems to have been written shortly after that to the Galatians. The concerns

'hich Paul displays here are still the same ones: estab-
shing that which distinguishes the new dispensation from
ıe ancient order—the now outdated Judaism. The
'hristian dispensation is a regimen of faith in Christ
isen from the dead, of life in the Spirit, and therefore
f participation in the sufferings of Christ in the well-
ounded hope of sharing in His glory:

> . . . Justified therefore by faith . . . we exult in the hope of the glory of the sons of God. . . . And hope does not disappoint, because the charity of God is poured forth in our hearts by the Holy Spirit who has been given to us (Rom. 5:1-5).

\ Christian is a new creature, dead, buried, and resur-
'ected with Christ thanks to his baptism, who serves God
letached from any Law and not only from the Jewish
Law which sought in vain to counteract the evil law of the
lesh.

> . . . In a new spirit and not according to the outworn letter (Rom. 7:6).

Chapter 7 of this Epistle is one of the most important for knowing the Spirit and His role, and also for knowing what a life subject to the Spirit must be. Paul here describes the life, free and full of hope, even if it unfolds in the midst of suffering, of those who are "moved by the Spirit," and whom the Spirit, even here below, makes into sons of God. It is a life of struggle and of suffering, for the Spirit must overcome the flesh within us (Rom. 7:14-25); it is, however, a blessed life which leads to glory:

> There is therefore now no condemnation for those who ar in Christ Jesus . . . for the law of the Spirit of the life i Christ Jesus has delivered me from the law of sin and o death. . . . they who are carnal cannot please God. You however, are not carnal but spiritual, if indeed the Spirit o God dwells in you. . . . If anyone does not have the Spiri of Christ, he does not belong to Christ . . . but if the Spirit o him who raised Jesus from the dead dwells in you, then h who raised Jesus Christ from the dead will also bring to lif your mortal bodies because of his Spirit who dwells in yo (Rom. 8:1-11).

All of Christian life, therefore, consists in resisting the flesh and in letting oneself be led by the Spirit who wants to make us sons of God:

> Therefore, brethren, we are debtors, not to the flesh, that we should live according to the flesh, for if you live according to the flesh you will die. But if by the spirit you put to death the deeds of the flesh, you will live. For whoever are led by the Spirit of God, they are the sons of God. Now you have not received a spirit of bondage so as to be again in fear, but you have received a spirit of adoption as sons, by virtue of which we cry, "Abba! Father!" The Spirit himself gives testimony to our spirit that we are sons of God. But if we are sons, we are heirs also: heirs indeed of God and joint heirs with Christ, provided, however, we suffer with him that we may also be glorified with him (Rom. 8:12-17).

This glorification the Spirit makes us want and hope for with constancy (Rom. 8:23-25). He makes us ask for it by stirring up our prayers and uniting with them, coming to the rescue of our weakness and impotence (Rom. 8:26-27).

3. THE SPIRIT OF HOLINESS

The framework of Old Testament thinking was also Paul's. The Holy Spirit is essentially the bearer of a new covenant and law. On Pentecost and subsequently in each faithful soul, Sinai is renewed but on the deeper and more interior level envisaged by Ezechiel. This level is even so much more profound, so different, that Paul, involved in his argument with the Judaizers, ended up stressing mainly that which distinguishes Sinai from the new Sion, rather than that which insures continuity.

The law of Sinai was, objectively, an ideal of holiness; but experience would emphasize man's inability to attain this ideal. Of course, the future law of Sion was going to permit the "saints" to attain this ideal, but this was only a messianic ideal. Also, when the Old Testament speaks of the "Holy Spirit" of God,[54] it is stressing above all His divine origin, but with nostalgia for a holiness far removed from man. But now Paul announces that the Holy Spirit is no longer only a spirit of "holiness" but of "sanctification," that He now communicates this holiness, that He sanctifies (2 Thess. 2:13; 1 Cor. 6:11; Eph. 5:15; cf. 1 Pet. 1:2). The new law is no longer merely a far-off ideal of holiness; of itself, it effects this holiness in man, it becomes sanctification. It is in this context that the Christian expression of the "Holy Spirit" was born, and this is what distinguishes the formula "Holy Spirit" in the Old Testament from our own.

[54] Cf. *supra*, p. 66ff.

4. THE FRUITS OF THE SPIRIT[55]

As a matter of fact, the new law is no longer just an external apparatus of virtues and good acts, but instead, through the action of the Spirit, it welds in us these virtues and good acts. To bring out the meaning of this new phenomenon, Paul turns to an image from the Old Testament. The good wind from the west, by bringing rain with it, fecundated the earth;[56] the spirit of God also fecundates the desert and transforms it into a paradise-like plantation when the people return to the Promised Land.[57] This is the paradise-and-Messias image to which Paul adheres, as early as 1 Thessalonians 4:8, where he cites Ezechiel 37:14. It will not leave him, and he will go on to speak of the "fruits" of the Spirit (Gal. 5:22), of the "harvests" of the Spirit (Gal. 6:8), or, more simply, of the "goods" of the Spirit (1 Cor. 9:11; Rom. 15:27), of His "gifts" (1 Cor. 12:1-13; 14:1-12; Rom. 1:11; cf. Heb. 2:4; 6:4).*

Among the principal "fruits" of the Spirit, Paul on several occasions emphasizes joy and peace (1 Thess. 1:6; Gal. 5:22; Rom. 14:17; 15:13). We are dealing here

[55] Cf. Viard, "Le fruit de l'Esprit," *Vie Spir*. 88, 1953, 451-470. This article, however, does not sufficiently come to grips with the question from the biblical point of view.

[56] Cf. *supra,* p. 13.

[57] Cf. *supra,* p. 15.

* TRANSLATOR'S NOTE: In some of these references, the word in question does not appear as such in the English version; however, the sense is clear enough.

vith two eschatological gifts proper to the Kingdom of he final ages distributed to Christians by the prophetic Spirit who arouses the enthusiasm of today's Christians ust as He roused the inspired men and women of old. It is interesting, moreover, to underline how much importance Luke attaches to joy as a gift of the Spirit. Nowhere do "joy" and "Spirit" re-appear more often than in Luke 1, 2 and Acts 2-4.

We must also indicate the fruits of *strength* and *patience* (Rom. 8:26; Eph. 3:14; 4:17; cf. 1 Pet. 4:14; 1 John 4:4-6). These fruits are justified in the context of the testimony and the opposition between the Spirit and the world of which we have already spoken. But the most important and most original fruit is *love* (Rom. 5:5; 1 Cor. 12:31; Eph. 3:16-17; Gal. 5:22; Rom. 15:30; cf. 1 John 3:23-24; 4:7-19). No longer is it a question merely of love for God or of love for one's neighbor, after the fashion of the old Law, but of the presence in us of the very love of God coming in some way to cap as well as to provide a base for both love for God and love among brethren.[58]

5. THE LAW GIVES PLACE TO THE SPIRIT[59]

Paul often uses such expressions as: you are "led" by the Spirit (Gal. 5:18; Rom. 8:14), you are "driven" by the

58 Cf. Debroches, "L'Esprit Saint, principe communautaire selon Saint Paul," *Vie Spir.* 75, 1946, 476-492; C. Charlier, "L'Amour en Esprit," *Bi. Vi. Ch.*, 1955, no. 10, 57-72.

59 Cf. Boismard, "La Loi et l'Esprit," *Lum. Vie.*, 1955, no. 21, 345-362.

Spirit (Gal. 5:16[60]).* While he is merely restating an old theme current in the primitive community and in the Acts, it is significant that he uses it primarily in those passages dealing with the new Covenant. In recalling through these images the action of the Spirit leading or driving the people in the desert (Ex. 14:21; 15:8-10; Is. 63:7-19), and then Christ in His turn (cf. Mark 1:12-13), Paul wishes to signify that this action in the desert of the Exodus is now carried out by the action of the Holy Spirit working in souls. However holy it might be, the ancient Law proved to be ineffective (Rom. 7:12), and still is for the carnal beings that we are (Rom. 7:14-16), for it touches only the mind and does not transform hearts (Rom. 3:20). From this viewpoint, the old Law is but death and condemnation (Gal. 3:10; 2 Cor. 3:6-9). It can only be proclaimed with a veil over one's eyes (2 Cor. 3:5-18). But now a new Law is given by a Spirit of life, the same that raised up the dead Christ (Rom. 8:1-4): there is, therefore, no longer any room for a law of death. And this new Law is given by a Spirit which glorified the Lord (2 Cor. 3:5-18): there is, then, no longer any room for the veiled Law.

[60] People have often drawn arguments from this terminology to affirm the personality of the Holy Spirit, who seems to act as a person. To be sure, this personality is unquestionable; however, it must be uncovered from more obvious texts. Here, it is quite simply a question of attributing, while spiritualizing, the action of the wind in Exodus and the return to the Promised Land, to the Holy Spirit, guide of the new people toward the true Promised Land through the influence of His suggestions and of His graces.

* TRANSLATOR'S NOTE: Here the Confraternity English version has "walk in the Spirit," which does not render the sense of the context. I have used a direct translation from the French text.

The life of the Christian no longer is the conforming of one's conduct to an external rule, but "docility" (Gal. 5:16) to the interior law of the Spirit who must not be "grieved" (Eph. 4:30; cf. Heb. 10:29; Jas. 4:5). This interior law is like a "fire" which burns everything that resists it and which must not be extinguished (1 Thess. 5:19), like a "wine" which must fill us with strength and inebriate us (Eph. 5:18; cf. Acts 2:13-21 and John 2:1-11).

To wish to live according to the rule of a purely external law is to deny the Spirit, against whose works there is no law (Gal. 5:22-23); it is to return to the "letter" which Paul opposes to the Spirit just as the flesh is opposed to Him, thus making his own the ancient coupling of the Old Testament (1 Cor. 6:9-11; 2 Cor. 3:2-18; Gal. 5:5-26; 6:7-8; Rom. 7:6; 8:8-17; cf. John 3:5-8; 1 Pet. 1:12).

Removed from the sway of a Law and of the law of the flesh, the Christian therefore enjoys the "freedom of the Spirit" (Gal. 4-5; Rom. 8).

6. CONCLUSION: THE SPIRIT OF ADOPTION OF SONS

In the two most important passages of Paul's pneumatology, the mystery of this new covenant through the Spirit, which sanctifies us of itself, without recourse to an external law, is clearly drawn. Both in Galatians 4 and in Romans 8,[61] Paul is led to unveil the source of this external law: the Spirit of adoption which makes us sons of God υἱοί—sons, not merely τέκνοι—children) and permits us to cry out "Abba, Father" (Gal. 4:6; Rom. 8:14). It is more or less in the unfavorable light of the slavery of the letter and of the flesh that Paul discovers the adoption of the Spirit; since He is a Spirit of freedom, we are no longer slaves, but children and sons. Another idea brought Paul to the same discovery, that of inheritance (Rom. 8:17). The Spirit of God, even in the Old Testament, is the basic element of the "last times," He it is who "led" the people into the Promised Land and brought them back from exile,[62] who obtains for them the Kingdom, the inheritance, the glory (2 Thess. 2:14; Gal. 6:8; Rom. 5:5). Of course, we have as yet only the "down payment" of this inheritance, the pledge of the Spirit (2 Cor. 1:22; 5:7; Eph. 1:14), but the mere fact of being led by the Spirit toward the inheritance establishes us in the status of heirs, and therefore, of sons:

> Through him [Christ] we . . . have access in one Spirit to the Father (Eph. 2:18).

[61] On Rom. 8, cf. Huby, "La vie dans l'Esprit d'après Saint Paul," *Rech. Sc. Rel.*, 1940, 5-39; on Gal. 4, cf. J. Fransen, "La liberté en Esprit," *Bi. Vi. Ch.*, 1956, no. 14, 6, 81.

[62] Cf. *supra*, p. 48.

D

the New Creation: the New Man

Let us return once again to the mystery of Easter and Pentecost, since the whole doctrine of the Holy Spirit is born in these events.

1. COMING TO LIFE OF THE NEW ADAM

While one tradition, to which we have already referred,[63] sees in the resurrection of Christ His messianic investiture, another tradition has seen therein the coming to life of the new Adam through the breathing into His body of the Holy Spirit, the replica of the "breath" transmitted to Adam (Gen. 2:7):

> Put to death indeed in the flesh, he was brought to life in the spirit . . . (1 Pet. 3:18).

[63] Cf. *supra*, p. 100.

This image was developed and explained by Paul. The resurrection of Christ made Him as it were a new Adam, animated by the Spirit who gives life, very different from the first Adam, endowed only with the breath of life:

> So also with the resurrection of the dead. . . . If there is a natural body, there is also a spiritual body. . . . "The first man, Adam, became a living soul"; the last Adam became a life-giving spirit. . . . Therefore, even as we have borne the likeness of the earthy [Adam], let us bear also the likeness of the heavenly [Adam] (1 Cor. 15:42-49; cf. 2 Cor. 5:17).

Thus, at the Resurrection, a Body received its breath, its "spirit,"[64] a new Adam received from God His existence in order to become the head of a new human lineage. But this animation is not as yet completed, but goes on unceasingly in the "body of Christ," as a consequence of the Resurrection.

2. THE BODY OF CHRIST AND THE SPIRIT

The occasion for this comparison was given to Paul by the discussions going on in Corinth. He had to place the Corinthians on guard against human wisdom and invite them to let themselves be guided by the gifts of the Spirit who filled them, like the Spirit in a body which He animates and unifies:

> You know that when you were Gentiles, you went to dumb idols according as you were led. Wherefore I give you to

64 One must be careful not to push this symbolism and make the Spirit the soul of Christ, cf. Festugière, "La trichotomie de 1 Th. V, 23 et la philosophie grecque," *Rech. Sc. Rel.* 1930, 385-415.

> understand that no one speaking in the Spirit of God says "Anathema" to Jesus. And no one can say "Jesus is Lord" except in the Holy Spirit. Now there are varieties of gifts, but the same Spirit; and there are varieties of ministries, but the same Lord; and there are varieties of workings [divine], but the same God, who works all things in all. Now the manifestation of the Spirit is given to everyone. . . . To one through the Spirit is given the utterance of wisdom . . . to another faith . . . to another the gift of healing . . . to another the working of miracles . . . but all these things are the work of one and the same Spirit, who allots to everyone according as he will. For as the body is one and has many members, and all the members of the body, many as they are, form one body, so also is it with Christ. For in one Spirit we were all baptized into one body, whether Jews or Gentiles, whether slaves or free, and we were all given to drink of one Spirit (1 Cor. 12:2-13).

To be sure, in this passage, the body is as yet only an image applied simply to Christ. But Paul will end by speaking directly of the animating of the body of Christ, which is the Church, by the Holy Spirit:

> One body and one Spirit . . . (Eph. 4:4; cf. 1:19-23; 4:1-16).

The Christian requirement therefore will be to put off the "old man" and put on the new man whom the Spirit has animated and continues to vivify within the Church:

> You are to put off the old man, which is being corrupted through its deceptive lusts. But be renewed in the spirit of your mind, and put on the new man, which has been created according to God in justice and holiness of truth (Eph. 4:21-23).

Thus, little by little, the part played by the Spirit in the life of the Church is specified. We have seen His collaboration in the establishing of the messianic kingdom, His indispensable role in the diffusion of love; here, now, He is the life-giving soul of the Body of the Church.

3. THE NEW BIRTH

To express this mystery of the creation of the new Adam, prolonged in us and in the Church, Paul speaks of "regeneration and renewal by the Holy Spirit" (Tit. 3:5). John prefers the expression "born of the Spirit":

> Amen, amen, I say to thee, unless a man be born again of water and the Spirit, he cannot enter into the kingdom of God. That which is born of the flesh is flesh; and that which is born of the Spirit is spirit. . . . The wind blows where it will, and thou hearest its sound but dost not know where it comes from or where it goes. So is everyone who is born of the Spirit (John 3:5-8).

John learned from Jesus that spiritual birth is a mysterious fact which is accomplished invisibly and secretly, as Nicodemus learned to his great astonishment.

4. THE RESURRECTION OF THE DEAD, NEW CREATION

If the animating of the new Adam is the doing of the Holy Spirit, if this animating is continued in the Body of the New Man which is the Church, it is logical that this will end in the general reanimating of bodies in the resurrection of the dead.

> What is sown a natural body rises a spiritual body. If there is

> a natural body, there is also a spiritual body. So also it is written, "The first man, Adam, became a living soul"; the last Adam became a life-giving spirit. But it is not the spiritual that comes first, but the physical, and then the spiritual (1 Cor. 15:44-46).
>
> If the Spirit of him who raised Jesus from the dead dwells in you, then he who raised Jesus Christ from the dead will also bring to life your mortal bodies because of his Spirit who dwells in you (Rom. 8:11; cf. Col. 5:4-5).

Just as Adam had received a breath of life which he transmitted to all his descendants, the risen Jesus possesses a life-giving breath which He wants to give to all men. Paul, on the subject of our own resurrection, recalls for us the theme of the glorified Jesus receiving the Spirit in order to transmit Him, and shows us the presence of the Spirit in us as a promise of our future resurrection. He will also soon speak of the presence of the Spirit in us as the pledge of our glory (2 Cor. 1:22; 5:7; Eph. 1:14).

This re-creation, copied after that which Ezechiel had described at the time of the exile (Ezech. 37), is carried out in the same manner by the Spirit of God, and also will really complete the creation of the new Adam and quiet the groans of all creation which awaits this renewal (Rom. 8:22-23; 2 Cor. 5:4-5).

5. RE-CREATION OF THE ENTIRE UNIVERSE

If Christ has truly been established by the Holy Spirit as the new Adam, then His lordship must actually be exercised over every man, so that He can deserve to be in truth the head of the new human lineage. There is nothing astonishing, therefore, about finding a certain insistence on the idea of the universality of the new creation.

a) *The gift of tongues*

At the time of the first manifestation of the Spirit, on Pentecost, a phenomenon of tongues occurred:

> There appeared to them parted tongues as of fire, which settled upon each of them (Acts 2:3).

At first glance, this is only an ecstatic phenomenon, such as would be produced at Corinth under the influence of the Spirit (1 Cor. 12:14) and to which the inspired ones of old were accustomed (1 Kings 10:5-6; 10-13; Joel 3:1-5).[65] But this spiritual charism receives a very precise interpretation in the text itself:

> [They] began to speak in foreign tongues, even as the Holy Spirit prompted them to speak. Now there were staying at Jerusalem devout Jews from every nation under heaven. And when this sound was heard, the multitude gathered and were bewildered in mind, because each heard them speaking in his own language (Acts 2:4-6).

This universality of the outpouring of the Spirit of the new Adam therefore clearly etsablished the taking in hand by the head of mankind of all men "from every nation under heaven." This Pentecost was an effective prelude to the apostolic preaching, extended throughout the whole world, and there is nothing more significant than to see the Holy Spirit specifically intervene to urge

[65] Lyonnet, *De glossolalia Pentecostes eiusque significatione,* V. Dom. 1944, 65-75.

the Apostles to universal preaching, as a way of spreading to all men the Spirit of the new Adam (Acts 10:17-19; 11:12; 13:2-4; 16:6-7; 8:29-30; 8:39, quoted above pp. 78-79). One has but to reread the descriptions left us by Paul of his own ministry in order to be convinced that the constant references to the Spirit found therein correspond to the fundamental theme of the universality of re-creation (1 Thess. 1:4-7; 1 Cor. 2:1-13; Rom. 15:15-19).

b) *The promise to Abraham, and the Spirit*

Paul speaks on several occasions of the Spirit of the promise (Gal. 3:14). This is not a vague reminder of the prophetic promises in general, but of the promise par excellence, that made to Abraham. Paul arrived at this idea of the promise of Abraham through opposition to the law of Moses. Even on that basis alone, the promise made to Abraham already deserved to be called the promise of the Spirit, in contrast to the covenant of the letter. But there is more: Paul calls the promise to Abraham the promise of the Spirit above all, because it heralds the fatherhood of Abraham over all nations:

> Christ redeemed us from the curse of the Law . . . that the blessing of Abraham might come to the Gentiles through Christ Jesus, that through faith we might receive the promise of the Spirit (Gal. 3:14; cf. Rom. 15:8).

Thus, the universality of the new creation is outlined in the promise, and in it, the Holy Spirit of Pentecost truly assumes a catholic function.

Is it possible to compare this catholicity of the Spirit with any Old Testament foreshadowings? The wind of God was already in contact with the peoples,[66] but only in order to destroy them by the breath of God's vengeance. However, this vengeance is, in reality, only a terrifying means for obtaining from the nations an acknowledgment of God's sovereignty. In substituting Himself for it, the Holy Spirit achieves the same results with greater sweetness and love.

[66] Cf. *supra*, p. 19.

Worship in Spirit

1. JUDAISM

In the Old Testament, the Spirit of God is very seldom linked to worship. To be sure, the artisans of the Tabernacle were clothed with the spirit (Ex. 28:3), but this had to do far more with a spirit of wisdom in directing the construction than with a true spirit of religion. The comparison between the spirit and water,[67] between the anointing and the spirit,[68] are, at first glance, the only indications we could possibly use. It is, rather, in Judaism that we must search for our data.

The sacrifice of the Temple, especially that defined by the school of Deuteronomy, is a rich man's sacrifice.

[67] Cf. *supra*, p. 48.

[68] Cf. *supra*, p. 41.

It is the Jewish farmer, proprietor of fertile land, who comes forth to give to God a part of the wealth acquired: first-fruits, tithes and holocausts. No matter how religious this procedure may be, it remains very material: an external offering of material goods, a quantitative offering which requires equating the quality offered with the sentiment experienced (cf. 3 Kings 8:62-66), a ministerial offering in which, especially after Ezechiel, the priests monopolized all the directly ritualistic actions, leaving the faithful in the exterior areas of the Temple.

Beginning with the exile, a characteristic event would transform this perspective and bring to light an opposing current. The Jew became a poor man, and, since he intended to retain his integrity on both the religious and national levels, this poverty became almost a necessity and a vocation. Moreover, the Temple was temporarily destroyed, and when it was rebuilt, people became aware that it was far-off and could not suffice to express the piety of Jews at some distance. Then, a new theology of worship developed: the Jew, poor now, will no longer offer quantitative sacrifices, which, besides, God disdains (Ps. 39:7; 50:16-19); for them, he will substitute his "contrite heart," his "sacrifice of praise," his "obedience" (cf. Abraham's sacrifice: Gen. 22:1-13). Thenceforth, it would be the interior sentiments and the fruit of one's moral attitudes which would serve as the matter for the new sacrifice.

In addition, because he could not go to the Temple as regularly as, in his piety, he might wish, the pious Jew came to give progressively more cultural value to the meetings of the Synagogue, simple catechism lessons of a very legalistic cast, which gradually became organized into a real liturgy of the proclaiming of the Word. Little by little, this new form of worship became opposed to the worship of the Temple, took on the fundamental motifs of the "sacrifice of praise," and of the "interior sacrifice." Hereafter, the Word of God, on one hand, and the response of moral fidelity and of praise which it engendered in the soul, constituted the matter of the new sacrifice. All that was needed for this "worship in spirit" to be definitively authenticated, at least among certain Jewish sects, was for an important segment of the priestly caste to abandon the Temple and adopt this spiritual liturgy in the community of Qumrân.

Of course, in this regard, no one spoke as yet of "worship in spirit," but the reality was there, and only the terminology remained to be discovered. Moreover, it is not impossible that the relationship between Spirit and Word which we have already been able to glimpse[69] was born in this climate of interior worship opposed to the Temple.

2. SPIRITUAL WORSHIP

In the light of what has just been said, it is easy to understand and to interpret the attacks which Christ directed in His lifetime against the Temple and its external worship.

[69] Cf. *supra*, p. 38.

From the earliest years of the Church, polemical discussion touched on this point—we have preserved Stephen's arguments on this subject (Acts 6:13; 7:44-53). This line of argument then passed into the primitive catechesis and ended up in the synoptic texts (Matt. 12:6; 21:12-16; 24:1-29; 26:61). Mark is even more sensitive to it than the other synoptics, since he maintains that the curtain of the formalistic Temple was rent at the moment the interior sacrifice of obedience of the Poor Man par excellence was consummated (Mark 15:38).

But in all this, nothing as yet permits us to discern the terminology we are looking for: *worship in Spirit.* Only John, at the close of the literary composition of the New Testament, finally specifies this terminology. In His conversation with the Samaritan woman (John 4:1-42), Jesus, after having announced the outpouring of the Spirit under the symbol of living water—thus taking up once more a traditional prophetic image relative to the gift of the Spirit (John 4:10-14)—proclaims that thenceforth "the hour is coming" when the earthly sanctuaries, even that of Jerusalem, will have lost their splendor; for the worship which shall be rendered the Father will be a wholly spiritual worship. This "hour," for John, is that of the gift of the Spirit thanks to the Passion of Jesus (John 7:37-39; 19:30), but in a certain fashion it has already arrived:

> The hour is coming, and is now here, when the true worshippers will worship the Father in spirit and in truth. For the Father also seeks such to worship him. God is spirit,

and they who worship him must worship in spirit and in truth (John 4:23-24).[70]

With this declaration, John ended the second section of his Gospel, which had begun with the evocation of the true Temple which is the body of the Lord (John 2:21).

3. THE SPIRITUAL TEMPLE IN VIRTUE

In the eyes of the primitive teaching, as we have just seen, the Body of Christ is the new Temple of God where is offered the spiritual sacrifice consisting of the obedience of Christ to His Father and of the salvation brought by the Father to His Son. It would fall to the author of the Epistle to the Hebrews to develop this idea of the new worship "in Spirit" celebrated in the very body of Christ.

> For if the blood of goats and bulls and the sprinkled ashes of a heifer sanctify the unclean unto the cleansing of the flesh, how much more will the blood of Christ, who through the Holy Spirit offered himself unblemished unto God, cleanse your conscience from dead works to serve the living God (Heb. 9:13-14).

Just as the body of Christ became a spiritual temple through His obedience, so too the moral dispositions of every Christian will make of him a "spiritual temple." This idea was already found in the conclusion of the text we have just quoted, but is even more explicit in several passages of Paul:

[70] A commentary in terms of the overall Christian worship is found in Braun, "In spiritu et veritate," *Rev. thom.*, 1952, 245-274 and 485-507.

> Do you not know that you are the temple of God and that *the Spirit of God dwells in you*? If anyone destroys the temple of God, him will God destroy; for holy is the temple of God, and this temple you are (1 Cor. 3:16-17).

> Do you not know that your members are the *temple of the Holy Spirit*, who is in you, whom you have from God, and that you are not your own? For you have been bought at a great price. Glorify God and bear him in your body (1 Cor. 6:19-20; cf. also Eph. 2:19-22; Phillip. 3:3).

In Paul's view, the Spirit who now dwells in this new Temple replaces the "Glory" which inhabited the ancient Temple. But this Spirit is precisely the one who has sealed afresh the new alliance and bears in our souls the "fruits of the Spirit." Also, for Paul, the ceremonial of this new spiritual worship is nothing other than the practice of the virtues. The latter are, henceforth, the only sacrificial matter acceptable to God. This is why he uses each of the texts we have just quoted as the conclusion of a passage on the moral commitments of the Christian.

Peter, for his part, described this spiritual temple which is the holy Church, where the altar and the priesthood offer up the "spiritual sacrifice" of good actions:

> Be you yourselves as living stones, built thereon into a spiritual house, a holy priesthood, to offer spiritual sacrifices acceptable to God through Jesus Christ (1 Pet. 2:5).

4. THE SPIRIT WHO PRAYS FOR US

If the spiritual Temple is built on the covenant which the Spirit enters into in the soul of each person, its worship is also expressed in prayer. The latter consisted, in the primitive liturgy, of readings and hymns, and these were so much in contrast with the ancient liturgy of the Temple that Paul calls them spiritual songs (Eph. 5:19;[71] Col. 3:16), so spiritual, moreover, that often the Holy Spirit directly inspired their text and melody.

It seems clear that beginning with this experience, the primitive catechesis often associated prayer and the Holy Spirit. Already when Christ prays, He does so in the Spirit, in the view of the "liturgist" Luke:

> In that very hour he rejoiced in the Holy Spirit and said, "I praise thee, Father, Lord of heaven and earth, that thou didst hide these things from the wise and prudent, and didst reveal them to little ones. Yes, Father, for such was thy good pleasure. All things have been delivered to me by my Father; and no one knows who the Son is except the Father, and who the Father is except the Son, and him to whom the Son chooses to reveal him (Luke 10:21-22; cf. Jude 20).

But the Spirit, let us not forget, is the Spirit of the last times. He will, moreover, especially favor the prayer of those Christians who are awaiting the return of the Lord and the completion of the spiritualization of Christ's Mystical Body.

According to the Apocalypse, the Spirit unites with the prayer of the Church to call urgently for the return of Christ as avenger and redeemer of the saints:

> And the Spirit and the bride say, "Come!" And let him who hears say, "Come!" (Apoc. 22:17).

71 To be compared with Eph. 5:2 and ff., where the doctrine of the moral sacrifice is spelled out.

Paul was particularly sensitive to the eschatological scope of the prayer of the Spirit, for He it is who has placed in us the pledge of the good things for which we hope:

> We ourselves also who have the first-fruits of the Spirit—we ourselves groan within ourselves, waiting for . . . the redemption of our body. . . . But . . . the Spirit also helps our weakness. For we do not know what we should pray for as we ought, but the Spirit himself pleads for us with unutterable groanings. And he who searches the hearts knows what the Spirit desires, that he pleads for the saints according to God (Rom. 8:23-27).

Also, prayer in the Spirit is that which demands of God the total gift of the Spirit. It would seem that the Spirit of God groans within us, with us, until the moment when He can fully shine forth by raising us from the dead, by glorifying us, by bringing us moral sanctity and introduction to the eschatological kingdom. And so the prayer which is expressed through the Spirit has as its object the Spirit Himself.

This idea was already present in the teaching of Luke. Whereas the other synoptics say that the Father will give us "the good things" we ask for (Matt. 7:11), Luke speaks of the Holy Spirit Himself:

> Therefore, if you, evil as you are, know how to give good gifts to your children, how much more will your heavenly Father give the Good Spirit to those who ask him? (Luke 11:13).

In effect, Luke again associates the coming of the Spirit with prayer, and the fact that Pentecost is linked with the preceding prayer of the Apostles (Luke 11:13; Acts 1:14) is not accidental. For John, it is Christ Himself who complies with this law by praying to the Father to send His Spirit (John 14:13-14).

Thus, once again, we must seek in the paschal mystery the final cause of this association between the Spirit and prayer. Indeed, just as the Father responded to the spiritual sacrifice of His Son by sending in Him His resuscitating Spirit, so too does the Father animate in us, through the Spirit, the interior sacrifice we offer in suffering and in moral commitment; He responds to this spiritual sacrifice by the gradual sending of the Spirit who brings us little by little back to life, who glorifies us in hope, and deposits in us the first-fruits of a salvation which He Himself is eager to see accomplished.

5. THE SPIRIT WHO SPEAKS FOR US

The new liturgy of the spiritual Temple consists not merely of "spiritual offerings," of "hymns and prayers in the Spirit," but also of the proclaiming of God's Word. It must be noted here that it is the proclamation of the Scriptures in the liturgy, both of the synagogue and of the Christian church, which fixed the canon of the inspired books: what is read in the spiritual liturgy is inspired by the Spirit. Thus, as Peter says:

> No prophecy of Scripture is made by private interpretation. For not by will of man was prophecy brought at any time; but holy men of God spoke as they were moved by the Holy Spirit (2 Pet. 1:20-21).

> [The prophets] searched what time or circumstances the Spirit of Christ in them was signifying, when he foretold the sufferings of Christ, and the glories that would follow. To them it was revealed that not to themselves but to you they mere ministering those things which now have been declared to you by those who preached the gospel to you by the Holy Spirit sent from heaven (1 Pet. 1:10-12).

John similarly associated the Gospel message with the inspiration of the Holy Spirit, to the point that, in his view, to refuse the Gospel is to refuse the Spirit and to commit the unforgivable sin which the synoptics already had mentioned:[72]

> He who comes from heaven is over all. And he bears witness to that which he has seen and heard, and his witness no one receives. He who receives his witness has set his seal on this, that God is true. For he whom God has sent speaks the words of God, for not by measure does God give the Spirit. The Father loves the Son, and has given all things into his hand. He who believes in the Son has everlasting life; he who is unbelieving towards the Son shall not see life, but the wrath of God rests upon him (John 3:31-36).

6. THE SIGNS OF THE SPIRIT

All liturgy is organized around signs and rites. Worship in the Spirit, in its turn, will have its own signs and rites to evoke the action of the Spirit in creating the assembly of the saved.

a) *The mark of the saved: the seal of the Spirit*

The theme of the seal of the Spirit first comes up in the Second Epistle to the Corinthians:

[72] Matt. 12:27-32.

> Now it is God who is warrant for us and for you in Christ, who has anointed us, who has also stamped us with his seal and has given us the Spirit as a pledge in our hearts (2 Cor. 1:21-22).

Again, to the Ephesians, even more explicitly:

> And in him you too, when you had heard the word of truth, the good news of your salvation, and believed in it, were sealed with the Holy Spirit of the promise, who is the pledge of our inheritance, for a redemption of possession, for the praise of his glory (Eph. 1:13-14; cf. 4:30).

Seen in its biblical context, this expression, "seal of the Spirit," is self-explanatory.

Here are the Jews, mistreated in Egypt: God "marks" them with the blood of a Lamb in view of the coming liberation (Ex. 12:13). Then, the exiles condemned to expatriation: God, however, "marks" them with a cross to designate those among His people who would escape the final torments (Ezech. 9:4-7). Finally, we have the faithful delivered up to the miseries of a world in decline, but again, a "mark" reserves and sets apart those who will be liberated therefrom (Apoc. 7:3). The seal of the Spirit is, therefore, the mark which the Christian bears in his heart and which destines him to leave behind the woes of the world and to share, at some future date, in the eschatological deliverance. As such, the seal of the Spirit replaces the former mark borne by the Jews in their flesh (thus we note a new application of the flesh-spirit opposition):

> For we are the circumcision, we who serve God in spirit, who glory in Christ Jesus and have no confidence in the flesh (Phil. 3:3).

Thus, the seal is the sign of our being set apart for the kingdom to come, of our assurance that we will be completely liberated on the day of glory. And who, better than the Spirit, could take the responsibility of impressing this mark upon us, He who is charged with preparing the kingdom of the final times? This explains why, for Paul, "seal" and "pledge" are practically synonymous.

b) *The living water of the Spirit*

From the time of the first Pentecost, the gift of the Holy Spirit is linked with a baptism of water, a baptism distinct from and richer than that of the Baptist, precisely because it brings the Holy Spirit with it (cf. Acts 19:1-7):

> Repent and be baptized every one of you in the name of Jesus Christ for the forgiveness of your sins; and you will receive the gift of the Holy Spirit (Acts 2:38).

The bond between the Spirit and the water of Baptism seems so close that they hasten to baptize anyone who might have received the Spirit in an unexpected manner:

> Can anyone refuse the water to baptize these, seeing that they have received the Holy Spirit just as we did? (Acts 10:47).

Toward the end of the period of apostolic catechesis, in one of the last texts committed to writing, Baptism is directly linked to the Holy Spirit:

> Go, therefore, and make disciples of all nations, baptizing them in the name of the Father, and of the Son, and of the Holy Spirit (Matt. 28:19).

And Paul, at the end of his own teaching, arrived at the same relationship between Baptism and the Spirit:

> We ourselves also were once unwise, unbelieving, going astray, slaves to various lusts and pleasures, living in malice and envy, hateful and hating one another. But when the goodness and kindness of God our Savior appeared, then not by reason of good works that we did ourselves, but according to his mercy, he saved us through the bath of regeneration and renewal by the Holy Spirit; whom he has abundantly poured out upon us through Jesus Christ our Savior, in order that, justified by his grace, we may be heirs in the hope of life everlasting (Tit. 3:3-7).

John reflected on these things and put them within his own particular perspective. On the one hand, he went beyond the narrow framework of a rite of water to join the Holy Spirit to the very theme of water, as it appears in the Bible,[73] and, on the other, he applied to the fleshly Christ what Paul, before him, had reserved solely to the spiritual and glorified Christ.

We see this, for example, at the Feast of the Tabernacles, in Jerusalem. This feast included prayers to obtain rain and the fertility of the fields, and processional rituals of water and libation accompanied these prayers. The ritual, as such, was quite pagan, and an attempt had been made to give it a meaning more in keeping with the Scripture. Care was taken especially to recall the miracle of the rock of living water in the desert (Ex. 17:1-7; Num.

73 Cf. Braun, "L'eau et l'Esprit," *Rev. thom.*, 1949, 5-30.

20:8; Is. 48:21; Ps. 104:41). Then, in order to give this past event a messianic coloration, a prophetic theme such as that of the water which issued from the side of the Temple in Ezechiel 47:1-12, was probably added, all the more readily since the rock of the living water in the desert was believed to have followed the Jews in their wanderings (cf. 1 Cor. 10:3, which speaks of this "spiritual" rock), finally ending up on the very site of the Temple. In the midst of all this, Jesus, who was staying away from Judea because the Jews were seeking to put Him to death, returned to Jerusalem during the feast. On the last day of the feast, Jesus again announced the gift of the living water of which He had already spoken to the woman of Samaria, and John explains for us the meaning of the Lord's words as it appeared in full to him after the gift of the Spirit and the sacrifice of Jesus:

> Now on the last, the great day of the feast, Jesus stood and cried out, saying, "If anyone thirst, let him come to me and drink. He who believes in me, as the Scripture says, 'From within him there shall flow rivers of living water'." He said this, however, of the Spirit whom they who believed in him were to receive; for the Spirit had not yet been given, since Jesus had not yet been glorified (John 7:37-39).

The phrase "from within him there shall flow rivers of living water," in the opinion of numerous exegetes, relates to Christ Himself who intends to present Himself, in the course of a feast oriented toward the ancient rock of living waters, as the true rock of living water. It is, therefore, really the announcement of a gift of the Spirit which will replace the former gift of living water and will prolong it until the fulfilment. Indeed, the rock of the new living water will pour forth this water at the same time as it gives the Spirit:

> One of the soldiers opened his side with a lance, and immediately there came out blood and water (John 19:34).

In thus linking water with the Spirit, John was unquestionably thinking of the baptismal rite, but he immediately went beyond it by placing it in the context which had, in the Old Testament, presided over the relationship between water and the Spirit. The miracle of the water gushing forth in the desert had already been attributed to the Spirit in the Jewish tradition, and the water which accordingly issues forth is but the image of messianic fruitfulness.[74] If there exists a ritual of water which communicates the Spirit, it can only be a rite of introduction to that new age which will be fulfilled in Paradise and is now being fashioned through the sacraments, represented here by the water.

c) *Water, blood, and the Spirit*

Each time John sets up the comparison between water and the Spirit, he adds to it a third element, forming a triad: blood. We saw this in the last text quoted above (John 19:34). It is even clearer in his first Epistle:

> This is he who came in water and in blood, Jesus Christ; not in the water only, but in the water and in the blood. And it is the Spirit that bears witness that Christ is the truth. For there are three that bear witness: the Spirit, and the water, and the blood; and these three are one (1 John 5:6-8).

[74] Cf. *supra*, p. 48.

Water and blood are thus the visible signs of the gif of the Spirit, and none of these gifts or signs is conferre without an absolute connection with the passion of Chris itself. In a closely related symbolism, the wedding a Cana and the changing of water into wine (blood) are seen from the same perspective (John 2:1-10).

d) *Baptism in fire and the Spirit*[75]

The synoptic tradition has preserved the memory of another sign of the Spirit: baptism with fire:

> I indeed baptize you with water, for repentance. But he who is coming after me is mightier than I, whose sandals I am not worthy to bear. He will baptize you with the Holy Spirit and with fire (Matt. 3:11).

This avowal by John the Baptist was duly preserved in the primitive tradition, especially at the time of the conflicts which arose between Christians and Johannites (cf. Acts 19: 1-7). In the opposition between the baptism of water and the baptism (in the ritual sense?) with the Spirit and with fire, one must see above all the contrast between a ritual which pacifies and prepares, and the ritual par excellence of introduction to the final ages, for fire and the Spirit have shared this feature of proclaiming the last times ever since, in the Old Testament, the burning wind of the desert served as the prime weapon, by day, for Yahweh.[76] Baptism in fire and the

[75] Cf. Edsman, *Le baptême de feu*, Upsala, 1940; Hamman, "Le baptême de feu," *Mél. Sc. Rel.*, 1951, 285-292.

[76] Cf. *supra*, p. 19.

pirit therefore designates entry into the last things—elebrated in particular through Christian Baptism—and, n that basis, it completely coincides with the outpouring f water and the Spirit described by John as the rite of nitiation into the messianic riches. In this regard, the aptism of fire in Matthew 3:11 is similar to the baptism of water in John. The image may have changed, since ohn can permit himself to be less concerned with the rgument, thenceforth terminated, with the Johannites, out the reality is the same: baptized with water or with ire, one enters the period of the fulfilment of God's plan.

e) *The anointing of the Spirit*

The New Testament writings do not describe a ritual of anointing which would communicate the Spirit. Only Baptism is mentioned, and we have seen that this "Baptism" must not necessarily be understood only of the actual ritual of water, but may indeed encompass a whole series of initiation rites.

But the idea of anointing in the Spirit remains quite alive. This is the very meaning which God gives to the reanimation of Christ at the time of His resurrection and messianic investiture:

> God anointed Jesus of Nazareth with the Holy Spirit and with power (Acts 10:38).

Paul took up this image, applying it rather vaguely to the Christian initiation:

> It is God . . . who has anointed us, who has also stamped us with his seal (2 Cor. 1:21-22).

Once again here, we need not ask ourselves whethe
Paul was thinking of a Christian ritual of anointing. It
certain that he was thinking of the anointing promised t
the future Messias, which actually did flow on Him at th
time of His messianic investiture, whether it was that c
the Resurrection or that of the baptism in the Jordan.

It is also certain that this messianic anointing wa
transferred by Paul from the Messias to all His faithfu
people. Each of them becomes a "Messias" in his turn
in the threefold dimension of priesthood, kingship, an
prophethood (cf. 1 Pet. 2:9-10; Apoc. 1:6; 5:10; 20:6)
Nor is the fact that the anointing, heretofore jealousl
monopolized by kings and priests, now becomes somehow
democratically distributed through all the people, the
least of the marvels of the age ruled by the Spirit. Henceforth, worship in the Spirit will no longer be that of a
sacerdotal caste, leaving the laity behind in the outer
courts; it will be the worship of the community as such,
structured to be sure, but all of it the active depository of
the royal priesthood of the Messias.

f) *The imposition of hands*

While the whole community of the elect is now the trustee of this messianic priesthood, as an extension of the priesthood of the Messias and of the anointing He received for this purpose from the Holy Spirit, it nevertheless remains true that this ideal will only attain its perfection in the worship of heaven. In the Church's long march, ministerial functions are still necessary. The Holy

›irit still rules and confers these functions by a ritual; ıt now one does not speak of an anointing reserved to ıe messianic worship. A new ritual is adopted for this 'pe of investiture: the laying on of hands. In this way, :ven deacons are entrusted with functions in Jerusalem \cts 6:6), and two Apostles enter upon their mission:

> The Holy Spirit said, "Set apart for me Saul and Barnabas unto the work to which I have called them." Then, having fasted and prayed and laid their hands upon them, they let them go (Acts 13:2-3).

\lso, it is by means of this ritual that Paul established he first elements of the hierarchy:

> For this reason I admonish thee to stir up the grace of God which is in thee by the laying on of my hands. For God has not given us the spirit of fear, but of power and of love and of prudence (2 Tim. 1:6-7).

Without, perhaps, being quite so "sacramental," ıevertheless, the laying of Ananias' hands on Saul—"That hou mayest recover thy sight and be filled with the Holy 5pirit" (Acts 9:17)—rightfully fits into this nomenclature.

7. CONCLUSION: BAPTISM AND CONFIRMATION

A spiritual Temple prolongs on earth that perfect Temple which was the body of Christ on the Cross. Three essential components regulate the ceremonials of the new liturgy. Henceforth, the whole people are priest and king and prophet, and thus heir to the messianic powers Christ

acquired through His investiture. This royal priesthood
exercised chiefly by interior sacrifice and obedience t
the Law which the Spirit suggests to our hearts. Accor
ingly, the Covenant is no longer a contract which con
mits us to obligations which are more or less external:
has become interior glorification and an authentic act c
worship. Finally, this worship in spirit is itself in evolu
tion: the Word which is proclaimed there and the groan
ing of the prayer expressed there are but the prelude t
the true spiritual liturgy—that of heaven. These thre
elements: royal priesthood of the faithful, sacrifice of th
heart, and eschatological scope, are each inaugurated b
a specific act of the Spirit empowering the faithful fo
the functions flowing therefrom: an anointing is neede
to assume the messianic priesthood; a renewal of th
Covenant is needed in order to be able to offer the spirit
ual victims; finally, one must be marked with the seal o
the Spirit in order to possess the pledge of the heavenly
liturgy.

In general, the Scriptures present these three acts of initiation under the overall expression "baptism," a concept generally broader than that of our present-day ritual of Baptism and even sometimes so broad that it encompasses the entire introduction to the age of the Holy Spirit (Acts 1:5). Within this general rite of Baptism, actions which seem closely connected and mutually complementary (Acts 19:2) are more or less clearly distinguished. Thus, there is immersion into the water on the one hand, and the laying on of hands, on the other.

he latter tends, quite vaguely, to be associated with the ift of the Spirit (Acts 8:14-24), but the Spirit can al-eady reveal Himself prior to this imposing of hands Acts 10:47). In any event, it is certain that this laying n of hands appears to be an exclusive monopoly of the postles (Acts 8:14-24; 19:6).

Let us leave to the theologians and historians of the nstitutions of the Church, the task of specifying the part layed by the Spirit in Baptism and Confirmation. For ıs, it is enough that we adopt the viewpoint of the New Testament in which the gift of the Spirit is made *in globo*, n a general rite of initiation.

𝒯

Conclusion: the Church and the Spirit

The Holy Spirit is the reanimating factor for Christ dead in the tomb. As such, He causes the Son of God to make the paschal "passage" from death to life, and leads Him to the Promised Land. Thus, the "Kingdom," heretofore merely sketched out or prophesied, by means of this intervention of the Holy Spirit on the person of Christ, becomes a reality. The last ages are inaugurated.

But this same Spirit who has introduced the son of man into this Kingdom is the one who makes us enter therein, and the paschal process in us is identical with the process in Christ. It differs only in the aspect of duration: what was done, once and for all, in Christ, is brought about only gradually in the Church. Yet all her members

e already marked in view of the day of fulness and of
e final access to the Kingdom.

The Holy Spirit is the agent of the creation of the
:w Adam. It is a new Man who emerges from the tomb
ı Easter Sunday, the first-fruits of a regenerated world
ı which unity is forged over and above all nations and
ıces through common filiation to the one Father. But
ıis re-creation, achieved at the outset in the person of the
ew Adam, continues progressively in men and in a
ʼorld which groans in the expectation of receiving the
ılness of its regeneration at the resurrection of the dead.
'he duration of the Holy Spirit's operation extends from
ne resurrection of Christ to the resurrection of the dead:
his is the time of the Church. The wind has brought
ain to the earth, the latter becomes fertile and will bear
ts fruit, but the time of fruitfulness is known only to the
ᶠather.

The Holy Spirit is the agent of the messianic investi-
ure of the risen Lord. Through the anointing of the
Spirit, Christ becomes Messias, in His royalty, His priesthood, and His prophetic mission; the Pentecost which has
radiated forth upon the Church since that time is but the
exercising of the messianic prerogatives of Christ, sublimated in His heavenly glorification.

One of the main characteristics of the exercise of
Christ's messianic privileges is that of communicating the
latter to the people itself. The Christian becomes a witness, the other facet of the prophet; he participates in the
royal priesthood of the messianic people in the offering of

the spiritual worship, he reigns with Christ over th powers of the world, especially in the victory which th Spirit wins over the flesh and over the law. The Church the community of the messianic riches sublimated an spiritualized through the action of the Holy Spirit.

In manifesting Himself on Pentecost evening, th Holy Spirit was bringing to mankind, in the name of it new Moses, standing now upon the spiritual Sinai, th new Law which transforms hearts and seals mankin in the love God bears it and which shines forth throug it. The glorification of Christ by the Spirit at the momen of His resurrection becomes the sanctification of Hi members throughout their lives.

The Church is this community of the sanctified mov ing to its total regeneration, the perfect replica of th glory of Christ, a people learning now to live this glor in the fruits of the Spirit and in the love which seals thei hearts.